New Testament
Men of Faith

New Testament
Men of Faith

F. B. MEYER

Good News Publishers
Westchester, Illinois

A NOTE ABOUT THE SCRIPTURE REFERENCES:
F. B. Meyer was so thoroughly familiar
with the Scriptures that he was accustomed
to draw on them from memory in his sermons
and books. The publishers have retained
Dr. Meyer's informal approach to quoting
Scripture so that none of the flavor and
immediacy of his unique writings will be
lost. For those who wish to read the Scriptures
he quotes from in context, or to see what
the exact wording of the texts is, we have
provided references.

Contents

BOOK I: JOHN THE BAPTIST

BOOK II: PETER

BOOK III: PAUL

BOOK I: JOHN THE BAPTIST

1
Schools and Schoolmasters

Luke 1

Zacharias and Elizabeth had probably almost ceased to pray for a child, or to urge the matter. There had been no heaven-sent sign to assure them that there was any likelihood of their prayer being answered, and nature seemed to utter a final No; when suddenly the angel of God broke into the com-monplace of their life, like a meteorite into the unrippled water of a mountain-sheltered lake, bringing the assurance that there was no need for fear, and the announcement that their prayer was heard. It must have been like hearing news that a ship, long overdue and almost despaired of, has sud-denly made harbor.

On his arrival in his home, the aged priest, by means of the writing table afterwards referred to, informed his wife, who apparently had not accompanied him, of all that had happened, even to the name which the child was to bear. She, at last, seems to have found no difficulty in accepting the divine assurance, and during her five months of seclu-sion she nursed great and mighty thoughts in her heart, in the belief and prayer that her child would become all that his name is supposed to signify, *the gift of Jehovah*. It was Elizabeth also who recognized in Mary the mother of her Lord, greeted her as blessed among women, and assured her that there would be for her a fulfilment of the things which had been promised her.

Month succeeded month; but Zacharias neither heard nor

spoke. His friends had to make signs to him, for unbelief has the effect of shutting man out of the enjoyment of life, and hindering his usefulness. How different this time of waiting from the blessedness it brought to his wife's young relative, who believed the heavenly messenger. He was evidently a good man and well versed in the history of his people. His soul, as we learn from his song, was full of noble pride in the great and glorious past. He could believe that when Abraham and Sarah were past age, a child was born to *them,* who filled their tent with his merry prattle and laughter; but he could not believe that such a blessing could fall to his lot. And is not that the point where our faith staggers still? We can believe in the wonderworking power of God on the distant horizon of the past, or on the equally distant horizon of the future; but that He should have a definite and particular care for *our* life, that *our* prayers should touch Him, that He should give *us* the desire of our heart—this staggers us, and we feel it is too good to be true.

His lowly dwelling was one day crowded with an eager and enthusiastic throng of relatives and friends. They had gathered to congratulate the aged pair, to perform the initial rite of Judaism, and to name the infant boy that lay in his mother's arms. Ah, what joy was hers when they came to "magnify the Lord's mercy towards her, and to rejoice with her!" As the people passed in and out, there was a new glow in the brilliant eastern sunlight, a new glory on the familiar hills.

In their perplexity at the mother's insistence that the babe's name should be John—none of his kindred being known by that name—they appealed to his father, who with trembling hand inscribed on the wax of the writing tablet the verdict, "His name is John." So soon as he had broken the iron fetter of unbelief in thus acknowledging the fulfilment of the angel's words, "his mouth was opened immediately, and his tongue loosed, and he spake, blessing God. And fear came on all that dwelt round about them." All these sayings quickly became the staple theme of conversation throughout all the hill country of Judea; and wherever they came, they excited the profoundest expectation. People laid them up in their hearts, saying, "What, then, shall this child be?"

"And the child grew, and waxed strong in spirit" (v. 80). "And the hand of the Lord was with him."

There were several remarkable formative influences operating on this young life.

His father was a priest. John's earliest memories would register the frequent absence of his father in the fulfilment of his course; and, on his return, with what eagerness would the boy drink in a recital of all that had transpired in the Holy City! We can imagine how the three would sit together beneath their trellised vine, in the soft light of the fading sunset, and talk of Zion, their chief joy. No wonder that in after days, as he looked on Jesus as He walked, he pointed to Him and said, "Behold the Lamb of God"; for, from the earliest, his young mind had been saturated with thoughts of sacrifice.

When old enough his parents would take him with them to one of the great festivals, where, amid the thronging crowds, his boyish eyes opened for the first time upon the stately Temple, the order and vestments of the priests, the solemn pomp of the Levitical ceremonial. The young heart dilated and expanded with wonder and pride.

He would be also taught carefully in the *Holy Scriptures*. Like the young Timothy, he would know them from early childhood. What would we not have given to hear Zacharias quote Isaiah 40 or Malachi 3, and turn to the lad at his knee, saying, "These words refer to thee":

"Yea, and thou, child, shalt be called the Prophet of the Most High; for thou shalt go before the face of the Lord to prepare His ways."

Sometimes when they were abroad together in the early dawn, and saw the first peep of day, the father would say: "John, do you see that light breaking over the hills? What that dayspring is to the world, Jesus, thy cousin at Nazareth, will be to the darkness of sin." Then, turning to the morning star, shining in the path of the dawn, and paling as they gazed, he would say: "See thy destiny, my son: I am an old man, and shall not live to see thee in thy meridian strength; but thou shalt shine for only a brief space, and then decrease, while He shall increase from the faint flush of dayspring to the perfect day." And might not the child reply, with a flash of intelligent appreciation?—"Yes, father, I understand; but I shall be satisfied if only I have prepared the way of the Lord."

The angel, who announced his birth, foretold that he should drink neither wine nor strong drink from his birth, but that he should be filled with the Holy Spirit. "John," said our Lord, "came neither eating nor drinking" (Luke 7:33). This abstinence from all stimulants was a distinct sign of the Nazarite, together with the unshorn locks, and the care with which he abstained from contact with death. In some cases, the vow of the Nazarite might be taken for a time, or, as in the case of Samson, Samuel, and John, it might be for life. But, whether for shorter or longer, the Nazarite held himself as peculiarly given up to the service of God, pliant to the least indication of His will, quick to catch the smallest whisper of His voice, and mighty in His strength.

"Mother, why do I wear my hair so long? You never cut it, as the mothers of other boys do."

"No, my son," was the proud and glad reply; "you must never cut it as long as you live: *you are a Nazarite.*"

"Mother, why may I not taste the grapes? The boys say they are so nice and sweet. May I not, next vintage?"

"No, never," his mother would reply; "you must never touch the fruit of the vine: *you are a Nazarite.*"

If, as they walked along the public way, they saw a bone left by some hungry dog, or a little bird fallen to the earth to die, and the boy would approach to touch either, the mother would call him back to her side, saying, "Thou must never touch a dead thing. If thy father were to die, or I, beside thee, thou must not move us from the spot, but call for help. Remember always that thou art separated unto God; His vows are upon thee, and thou must let nothing, either in symbol or reality, steal away His power from thy young heart and life."

The effect of this would be excellent. It would give a direction and purpose to the lad's thoughts and anticipations. He realized that he was set apart for a great mission in life. The brook heard the call of the sea. Besides which, he would acquire self-restraint, self-mastery.

What is it to be "strong in spirit?" The man who carries everything before him with the impetuous rush of his nature, before whose outbursts men tremble, and who insists in all things on asserting his wild, masterful will—is he the strong man? Nay! Most evidently he must be classed among the weaklings. The strength of a man is in proportion to the feelings which he curbs and subdues and not which subdue him. The man who receives a flagrant insult, and answers quietly; the man who bears a hopeless daily trial, and remains silent; the man who with strong passions remains chaste, or with a quick sense of injustice can refrain himself and remain calm—these are strong men; and John waxed strong, because, from the earliest dawn of thought, he was taught the necessity of refusing things which in themselves might have been permissible, but for him were impossible.

On each of us rests the vow of separation, by right of our union with the Son of God, who was holy, harmless, undefiled, and separate from sinners. Remember how He went without the camp, bearing our reproach; how they cast Him forth to the death of the cross; and how He awaits us on the Easter side of death—and surely we can find no pleasure in the world where He found no place. His death has made a lasting break between His followers and the rest of men. They are crucified to the world, and the world to them.

But while we put away all that injures our own life or the lives of others, let us be very careful to discriminate, to draw the line where God would have it drawn, exaggerating and extenuating nothing. It is important to remember that while the motto of the old covenant was Exclusion, even of innocent and natural things, that of the new is Inclusion. Moses, under the old, forbade the Jews having horses; but Zechariah said that in the new they might own horses, only "Holiness to the Lord" must be engraven on the bells of their harness. Christ has come to sanctify all life. Whether we eat, or drink, or whatever we do, we are to do all to His glory. Disciples are not to be taken out of the world, but kept from its evil. "Every creature of God is good, and nothing to be refused, if it be received with thanksgiving; for it is sanctified by the Word of God, and prayer." Natural instincts are not to be crushed, but transfigured.

This is the great contrast between the Baptist and the Son of Man. The Nazarite would have felt it a sin against the law of his vocation and office to touch anything pertaining to the vine. Christ began His signs by changing water into wine, though of an innocuous kind, for the peasant's wedding at Cana of Galilee. John would have lost all sanctity had he touched the bodies of the dead, or the flesh of the leper. Christ would touch a bier, pass His hands over the seared flesh of the leper, and stand sympathetically beside the grave of His friend. Thus we catch a glimpse of our Lord's meaning when He affirms that, though John was the greatest of women born, yet the least in the Kingdom of Heaven is greater than he.

"The child was in the deserts till the day of his showing unto Israel" (v. 80). Probably Zacharias, and Elizabeth also, died when John was quite young. But he had grown into adolescence, was able to care for himself, and "the hand of the Lord was with him."

Beneath the guidance and impulse of that hand he tore himself from the little home to go forth from the ordinary haunts of men, perhaps hardly knowing whither. There was a wild restlessness in his soul.

Fatherless, motherless, brotherless, sisterless—a lone man, he passed forth into the great and terrible wilderness of Judea, which is so desolate that the Jews called it the abomination of desolation. Travelers who have passed over and through it say that it is destitute of all animal life, save a chance vulture or fox. When Jesus was there some two or three years after, He found nothing to eat; the stones around mocked His hunger; and there was no company save that of the wild beasts.

In this great and terrible wilderness, John supported himself by eating locusts—the literal insect, which is still greatly esteemed by the natives—and wild honey, which abounded in the crevices of the rocks; while for clothing he was content with a coat of coarse camel's hair, such as the Arab women make still; and a girdle of skin about his loins. A cave, like that in which David and his men often found refuge, sufficed him for a home, and the water of the streams that hurried to the Dead Sea, for his beverage.

Can we wonder that under such a regimen he grew strong? We become weak by continual contact with our fellows. We sink to their level; we accommodate ourselves to their fashions and whims; we limit the natural developments of character in God's plan; we take on the color of the bottom on which we lie. But in loneliness and solitude, wherein we meet God, we become strong. God's strong men are rarely clothed in soft raiment, or found in king's courts.

Yes, and there is a source of strength beside. He who is filled and taught, as John was, by the Spirit, is strengthened by might in the inner man. All things are possible to him that believes. Simon Bar-Jona becomes Peter when he touches the Christ. The youths faint and are weary, and the young men utterly fall; but they that wait on the Lord renew their strength: they who know God are strong and do exploits.

2

The Prophet of the Highest

Luke 1

"Thou, child, shalt be called the Prophet of the Most High"
(v. 76)—thus Zacharias addressed his infant son, as he lay in
the midst of that group of wondering neighbors and friends.
What a thrill of ecstasy quivered in the words! A long period,
computed at four hundred years, had passed since the last
great Hebrew prophet had uttered the words of the Highest.
Reaching back from him to the days of Moses had been a
long line of prophets, who had passed down the lighted
torch from hand to hand. And the fourteen generations, during which the prophetic office had been discontinued, had
gone wearily. But now hope revived, as the angel's voice
proclaimed the advent of a prophet. Our Lord corroborated
his words when, in after days, He said that John had been a
prophet, and something more. "But what went ye out to
see?" He asked. "A prophet? Yea, I say unto you, and much
more than a prophet" (Luke 7:26).

The Hebrew word that stands for *prophet* is said to be
derived from a root signifying "to boil or bubble over," and
suggests a fountain bursting from the heart of the man into
which God had poured it. Prophecy means the forthtelling of
the Divine message. "God spake *in* the prophets" (Hebrews
1:1). And when they were conscious of His mighty moving
and stirring within, woe to them if they did not utter it in
burning words, fresh minted from the heart.

But as the voice of Old Testament prophecy ceased, with

its last breath it foretold that it would be followed, in the after time, by a new and glorious revival of the noblest traditions of the prophetic office. "Behold," so God spake by Malachi, "I will send you Elijah the prophet before the great and terrible day of the Lord come. And he shall turn the heart of the fathers to the children, and the heart of the children to their fathers; lest I come and smite the earth with a curse" (Mal. 4:5, 6).

From his childhood and upwards they had been reiterated in his ear by his parents, who would never weary of reciting them.

How often he would ponder the reference to himself in the great Messianic prediction, "Comfort ye, comfort ye My people, saith your God. . . . The voice of one that crieth, Prepare ye the way of the Lord; make straight in the desert a highway for our God . . ." (Isaiah 40:1, 3). There was no doubt as to the relevance of those words to himself (Luke 1:76, Matt. 3:3). And it must have unconsciously wrought mightily in the influence it wielded over his character and ministry.

There was, also, that striking anticipation by Malachi which directly suggested Elijah as his model. Had not Gabriel himself alluded to it, when he foretold that the predicted child would go before the Messiah, in the spirit and power of Elijah (Luke 1:17)? And again his statement was confirmed by our Lord in after days (Matt. 11:14).

But the mind of the Forerunner must also have been greatly exercised by *the lawlessness and crime* which involved all classes of his countrymen in a common condemnation. The death of Herod, occurring when John was yet a child had led to disturbances which afforded an excuse for the Roman occupation of Jerusalem. The scepter had departed from Judah, and the lawgiver from between his feet. The high priesthood was a mere forfeit in the deals of Idumean tetrarchs and Roman governors. The publicans were notorious for their exactions, their covetousness, their cheating and oppression of the people. Soldiers filled the country with violence, extortion, and discontent. The priests were hire-lings; the Pharisees were hypocrites; the ruling classes had set aside their primitive simplicity and purity, and were given up to the voluptuousness and license of the Empire. "Brood of vipers" was apparently not too strong a phrase to use of the foremost religious leaders of the day—at least, when used, its relevance passed without challenge.

Tidings of the evil that was overflowing the land like a deluge of ink were constantly coming to the ears of this eager soul, filling it with horror and dismay; and to this must be traced much of the austerity which arrested the attention of his contemporaries. The idea which lies beneath the fasting and privation of so many of God's servants, has been that of an overwhelming sorrow, which has taken away all taste for the pleasures and comforts of life. And this was the thought by which John was penetrated. On the one hand, there was his deep and agonizing conviction of the sin of Israel; and on the other, the belief that the Messiah must be nigh, even at the doors. Thus the pressure of the burden increased on him till he was forced to give utterance to the cry it extorted from his soul: "Repent, for the Kingdom of Heaven is at hand."

But in addition to these we must add *the vision of God,* which must have been specially vouchsafed to him while he sojourned in those lonely wilds.

This has ever been characteristic of the true prophet. He has been a seer. He has spoken, because he has beheld with his eyes, looked upon, and handled the very Word of God. The Divine Prophet spoke for all that had preceded Him: "We speak that which we know, and testify that we have seen."

In this way we may have some share. It is permitted to us also to see; to climb the Mount of Vision, and look on the glory of God in the face of Jesus Christ; to have revealed to us things that eye hath not seen, nor ear heard, nor the heart of man conceived. Let us remember that we are to be God's *witnesses* in the Jerusalem of the home, the Judea of our im-mediate neighbors, and to the uttermost parts of the earth of our profession or daily calling. God demands not advocates, but witnesses; and we must see for ourselves, before we can bear witness to others, the glory of that light still flushing our faces, and the accent of conviction minted in our speech.

3

The First Ministry of the Baptist

Luke 3

Thirty years had left their mark on the Forerunner. For many years John had been living in the caves that indent the limestone rocks of the desolate wilderness which extends from Hebron to the western shores of the Dead Sea.

At last the moment arrived for him to utter the mighty burden that pressed upon him, "Repent! the Kingdom of Heaven is at hand" (Matt. 3:2).

It was as though a spark had fallen on dry tinder. Instantly people began to flock to him from all sides. "There went out to him Jerusalem, and all Judea, and all the region around about Jordan" (Matt. 3:5).

He seems finally to have taken his stand not far from the rose-clad oasis of Jericho, on the banks of the Jordan. The population of the metropolis, familiar with the Temple services, and accustomed to the splendor of the palace; fishermen from the Lake of Gennesaret; dusky sons of Ishmael from the desert of Gilead; the proud Pharisee; the detested publican, who had fattened on the sorrows and burdens of the people—were there, together with crowds of ordinary people that could find no resting place in the schools or systems of religious thought of which Jerusalem was the center.

Many causes accounted for John's immense popularity. The office of the prophet was almost obsolete. The oldest man living at that time could not remember having seen a man who had ever spoken to a prophet.

Moreover, John gave such abundant evidence of sincerity—of reality. His independence of anything that this world could give made men feel that whatever he said was inspired by his direct contact with things as they literally are.

Above all, he appealed to their moral convictions, and, indeed, expressed them. The people knew that they were not as they should be. It is in his direct appeal to the heart and conscience that the servant of God exerts his supreme and unrivalled power. Though a man may shrink from the preaching of repentance, yet, if it tell the truth about himself, he will be irresistibly attracted to hear the voice that harrows his soul. John rebuked Herod for many things; but still the royal offender sent for him again and again, and heard him gladly.

It is expressly said that John saw many Pharisees and Sadducees coming to his baptism (Matt. 3:7). Their advent appears to have caused him some surprise. "Ye offspring of vipers, who warned you to flee from the wrath to come?" The strong epithet he used of them suggests that they came as critics; because they were unwilling to surrender the leadership of the religious life of Israel, and were anxious to keep in touch with the new movement, until they could sap its vitality, or divert its force into the channels of their own influence.

But it is quite likely that in many cases there were deeper reasons. *The Pharisees* were the ritualists and formalists of their day, who would wrangle about the breadth of a phylactery, and decide to an inch how far a man might walk on the Sabbath day; but the mere externals of religion will never permanently satisfy the soul made in the likeness of God. Ultimately it will turn from them with a great nausea and an insatiable desire for the living God. As for the *Sadducees*, they were the materialists of their time. The reaction of superstition, it has been said, is to infidelity; and the reaction from Pharisaism was to Sadduceeism. Disgusted and outraged by the trifling of the literalists of Scripture interpretation, the Sadducee denied that there was an eternal world and a spiritual state, and asserted that "there is no resurrection, neither angel, nor spirit" (Acts 23:8). But mere negation can never satisfy. The heart still moans out its sorrow under the darkness of agnosticism, as the ocean sighing under a starless midnight. Nature's instincts are more cogent than reason. It was hardly to be wondered at, then, that these two great classes were largely represented in the crowds that gathered on the banks of the Jordan.

The main burden of the Baptist's preaching was "The Kingdom of Heaven is at hand." To a Jew that phrase meant the reestablishment of the Theocracy, and a return to those great days in the history of his people when God Himself was Lawgiver and King.

Instead of dilating on the material glory of the Messianic period, far surpassing the magnificent splendor of Solomon, he insisted on the fulfilment of certain necessary preliminary requirements, which lifted the whole conception of the anticipated reign to a new level, in which the inward and spiritual took precedence over the outward and material. It was the old lesson, which in every age requires repetition, that unless a man is born again, and from above, he cannot see the Kingdom of God.

Be sure of this, that no outward circumstances, however propitious and favorable, can bring about true blessedness. We might be put into the midst of heaven itself, and be poor, and miserable, and blind, and naked, unless the heart were in loving union with the Lamb, who is in the midst of the throne. He is the light of that city, His countenance doth lighten it—from His throne the river of its pleasure flows, His service is its delightful business; and to be out of fellowship with Him would make us out of harmony with its joy. Life must be centered in Christ if it is to be concentric with all the circles of heaven's bliss. We can never be at rest or happy while we expect to find our fresh springs in outward circumstances. It is only when we are right with God that we are blest and at rest. And when all hearts are yielded to the King; when all gates lift up their heads, and all everlasting

doors are unfolded for His entrance—then the course which
has so long brooded over the world shall be done away. The
whole creation groaneth and travaileth for the manifestation
of the sons of God: but when they are revealed in all their
beauty, then judgment shall dwell in the wilderness, and
righteousness shall abide in the fruitful field; and the work of
righteousness shall be peace, and the effect of righteousness
quietness and confidence for ever; and the mirage shall become a pool, and the thirsty ground springs of water (Isa.
32:15, 16; 35:7).

Alongside the proclamation of the kingdom was the uncompromising insistence on *"the wrath to come."* John saw
that the Advent of the King would bring inevitable suffering
to those who were living in self-indulgence and sin.

At first Christ drew all men to Himself; but, as His ministry proceeded, He revealed their quality. A few were permanently attracted to Him; the majority were as definitely re-
pelled. There was no middle class. Men were either for or
against Him. The sheep on this side; the goats on that. The
five wise virgins, and the five foolish. Those who entered the
strait gate, and those who flocked down the broad way that
leadeth to destruction. So it has been in every age. Jesus
Christ is the touchstone of trial. Our attitude towards Him
reveals the true quality of the soul.

The fire of John's preaching had its primary fulfilment,
probably, in the awful disasters which befell the Jewish
people, culminating in the siege and fall of Jerusalem. We
know how marvelously the little handful of believers which
had been gathered out by the preaching of Christ and His
disciples were accounted worthy to escape all those things
that came to pass, and to stand before the Son of Man. But
the unbelieving mass of the Jewish people were discovered
to be worthless chaff and unfruitful trees, and assigned to
those terrible fires which have left a scar on Palestine to this
day.

But there was a deeper meaning. "He that believeth not
the Son shall not see life, but the wrath of God abideth on

him." The penalty of sin is inevitable. The wages of sin is death. The land which beareth thorns and thistles, after having drunk of the rain which cometh often upon it, is rejected and nigh unto a curse, its end is to be burned; under the first covenant, every transgression and disobedience received a just recompense of reward; the man that set at nought Moses' law died without compassion, on the word of two or three witnesses—of how much sorer punishment shall he be judged worthy who hath trodden under foot the Son of God, and hath counted the blood of the covenant a common thing, and hath done despite to the Spirit of grace!

Even if we grant, as of course we must, that many of the expressions referring to the ultimate fate of the ungodly are symbolical, yet it must be granted also, that they have counterparts in the realm of soul and spirit, which are as terrible to endure, as the nature of the soul is more highly organized than that of the body. Believe me when Jesus said, "These shall go away into eternal punishment," He contemplated a retribution so terrible, that it were good for the sufferers if they had never been born.

All John's preaching, therefore, led up to the demand for repentance. The word which was oftenest on his lips was "Repent ye!" It was not enough to plead direct descent from Abraham, or outward conformity with the Levitical and Temple rites. God could raise up children to Abraham from the stones of the river bed. There must be the renunciation of sin, the definite turning to God, the bringing forth of fruit meet for an amended life. In no other way could the people be prepared for the coming of the Lord.

4

Baptism Unto Repentance

Mark 1:4

At the time of which we are speaking, an extraordinary sect, known as the Essenes, was scattered throughout Palestine, but had its special home in the oasis of Engedi; and with the adherents of this community John must have been in frequent association. They were the recluses or hermits of their age.

The aim of the Essenes was moral and ceremonial purity. They sought after an ideal of holiness, which they thought could not be realized in this world; and therefore, leaving villages and towns, they betook themselves to the dens and caves of the earth, and gave themselves to continence, abstinence, fastings, and prayers, supporting themselves by some slight labors on the land. Those who have investigated their interesting history tell us that the cardinal point with them was faith in the inspired Word of God. By meditation, prayer, and mortification, frequent ablutions, and strict attention to the laws of ceremonial purity, they hoped to reach the highest stage of communion with God. They agreed with the Pharisees in their extraordinary regard for the Sabbath. Their daily meal was of the simplest kind, and partaken of in their house of religious assembly. After bathing, with prayer and exhortation they went, with veiled faces, to their dining room, as to a holy temple. They abstained from oaths, despised riches, manifested the greatest abhorrence of war and slavery, faced torture and death with the utmost bravery, refused the indulgence of pleasure.

It is clear that John was not a member of this holy community, which differed widely from the Pharisaism and Sadduceeism of the time. The Essenes wore white robes, emblematic of the purity they sought; while he was content with his coat of camel's hair and leathern girdle. They seasoned their bread with hyssop, and he with honey. They dwelt in brotherhoods and societies; while he stood alone from the earliest days of his career. But it cannot be doubted that he was in deep accord with much of the doctrine and practice of this sect.

John the Baptist, however, cannot be accounted for by any of the pre-existing conditions of his time. He stood alone in his God-given might. That he was conscious of this appears from his own declaration when he said, "He that sent me to baptize in water, He said unto me" (John 1:33). And that Christ wished to convey the same impression is clear from His question to the Pharisees: "The baptism of John, was it from heaven or from men?" (Luke 20:4). Moreover, the distinct assertion of the Spirit of God, through the fourth Evangelist, informs us: "There came a man, sent from God, whose name was John; the same came for witness, that *all* might believe through him" (John 1:6, 7). "The Word of God came unto John, the son of Zacharias, in the wilderness. And he came" (Luke 3:2).

John has a ministry with all men. In other words, he represents a phase of teaching and influence through which we must needs pass if we are properly to discover and appreciate the grace of Christ. With us, too, a preparatory work has to be done. There are mountains and hills of pride and self-will that have to be leveled; crooked and devious ways that have to be straightened; ruggednesses that have to be smoothed—before we can fully behold the glory of God in the face of Jesus Christ. In proportion to the thoroughness and permanence of our repentance will be our glad realization of the fulness and glory of the Lamb of God.

But we must guard ourselves here, lest it be supposed that repentance is a species of good work which must be performed in order that we may merit the grace of Christ. It must be made equally clear, that repentance must not be viewed apart from faith in the Savior, which is an integral part of it. It is also certain that, though "God commandeth all men everywhere to repent" (Acts 17:30), yet Jesus is exalted "to *give* repentance and the remission of sins."

It cannot be too strongly emphasized that repentance is an act of the *will*. In its beginning there may be no sense of gladness or reconciliation with God: but just the consciousness that certain ways of life are wrong, mistaken, hurtful, and grieving to God, and the desire, which becomes the determination, to turn from them, to seek Him who formed the mountains and created the wind, that maketh the morning darkness and treadeth upon the high places of the earth.

We need to turn from our own righteousness as well as from our sins. Augustine spoke of his efforts after righteousness as splendid sins; and Paul distinctly disavows all those attempts to stand right with God which he made before he saw the face of the risen Christ looking out from heaven upon his conscience-stricken spirit. You must turn away from your own efforts to save yourself. These are, in the words of the prophet, but "filthy rags." Nothing apart from the Savior and His work, can avail the soul, which must meet the scrutiny of eternal justice and purity.

There are signs and symptoms of repentance and confession is one. "They were baptized of him in the river Jordan, confessing their sins" (Matt. 3:6).

The formalist confessed that the whited sepulchre of his religious observances had concealed a mass of putrefaction. The sceptic confessed that his refusal of religion was largely due to his hatred of the demands of God's holy law. The multitudes confessed that they had been selfish and sensual, shutting up their compassions, and refusing clothing and food to the needy. The publican confessed that he had extorted by false accusation and oppression more than his due. The soldier confessed that his profession had often served as the cloak for terrorizing the poor and vamping up worthless accusations. The notoriously evil liver confessed that he had lain in wait for blood, and destroyed the innocent and helpless for gain or hate. The air was laden with the cries and sighs of the stricken multitudes, who beheld their sin for the first time in the light of eternity and of its inevitable doom. The lurid flames of "the wrath to come" cast their searching light on practices which, in the comparative twilight of ignorance and neglect, had passed without special notice.

Upon that river's brink, men not only confessed to God, but probably also to one another. Lifelong feuds were reconciled; old quarrels were settled; frank words of apology and forgiveness were exchanged; hands grasped hands for the first time after years of alienation and strife.

Confession is an essential sign of a genuine repentance, and without it forgiveness is impossible. "He that covereth his transgressions shall not prosper; but whoso confesseth and forsaketh them shall obtain mercy" (Prov. 28:13). "If we confess our sins, He is faithful and just to forgive us our sins, and to cleanse us from all unrighteousness" (I John 1:9). So long as we keep silence, our bones wax old through our inward anguish; we are burnt by the fire of slow fever; we toss restlessly, though on a couch of down. But on confession there is immediate relief. "I said, I will confess my transgressions unto the Lord, and Thou forgavest me the iniquity of my sin."

"Bring forth, therefore, fruit worthy of repentance," said John, with some indignation, as he saw many of the Pharisees and Sadducees coming to his baptism. He insisted that practical and vital religion was not a rule, but a life; not outward ritual, but a principle; not works, but fruit; and he demanded that the genuineness of repentance should be attested by appropriate fruit. "Do men gather grapes of thorns, and figs of thistles?" (Matt. 3:8; 7:16).

You will never get right with God till you are right with man. It is not enough to confess wrongdoing; you must be prepared to make amends so far as lies in your power. Sin is not a light thing, and it must be dealt with, root and branch.

"They were baptized . . . confessing their sins." "Purge me with hyssop, and I shall be clean. Wash me, and I shall be whiter than snow." They have longed to feel that as the body was delivered from pollution, so the soul was freed from stain. In some cases this thought has assumed a gross and material form; and men have attributed to the water of certain rivers, such as the Ganges, the Nile, the Abana, the mysterious power of cleansing away sin.

There was no trace of this, however, in John's teaching. It was not baptism *unto remission*, but *unto repentance*. It was the expression and symbol of the soul's desire and intention, so far as it knew, to confess and renounce its sins, as the necessary condition of obtaining the Divine forgiveness.

It meant death and burial as far as the past was concerned; and resurrection to a new and better future. Forgetting and dying to the things that were behind, the soul was urged to realize the meaning of this symbolic act, and to press on and up to better things before; assured as it did so that God had accepted its confession and choice, and was waiting to receive it graciously and love it freely.

It is easy to see how all this appealed to the people, and specially touched the hearts of young men. At that time, by the blue waters of the Lake of Galilee, there was a handful of ardent youths, deeply stirred by the currents of thought around them, who resented the Roman sway, and were on the tiptoe of expectation for the coming Kingdom. How they spoke together, as they floated at night in their fisherman's yawl over the dark waters of the Lake of Galilee, about God's ancient covenant, and the advent of the Messiah, and the corruptions of their beloved Temple service! And when, one day, tidings reached them of this strange new preacher, they left all and streamed with all the world beside to the Jordan valley, and stood fascinated by the spell of his words.

One by one, or all together, they made themselves known to him, and became his loyal friends and disciples. We are familiar with the names of one or two of them, who afterwards left their earlier master to follow Christ; but of the rest we know nothing, save that he taught them to fast and pray, and that they clung to their great teacher, until they bore his headless body to the grave. After his death they joined themselves with Him whom they had once regarded with some suspicion as his rival and supplanter.

How much this meant to John! He had never had a friend; and to have the allegiance and love of these noble, ingenuous youths must have been very grateful to his soul. But from them all he repeatedly turned his gaze, as though he were looking for some one who must presently emerge from the crowd; and the sound of whose voice would give him the deepest and richest fulfilment of his joy, because it would be the voice of the Bridegroom Himself.

5

The Manifestation of the Messiah

John 1:31

John's life, at this period, was an extraordinary one. By day he preached to the teeming crowds, or baptized them; by night he would sleep in some slight booth, or darksome cave. But the conviction grew always stronger in his soul, that the Messiah was near to come; and this conviction became a revelation. The Holy Spirit who filled him, taught him. He began to see the outlines of His Person and work.

He conceived of the coming King, as we have seen, as the Woodman, laying His axe at the root of the trees; as the Husbandman, fan in hand to winnow the threshing floor; as the Baptist, prepared to plunge all faithful souls in His cleansing fires; as the Ancient of Days, who, though coming after him in order of time, must be preferred before him in order of precedence, because He was before him in the eternal glory of His Being (John 1:15-30).

It was this vision of the Sun before the sunrise, as he viewed it from the high peak of his own noble character, that induced in the herald his conspicuous and beautiful humility. He insisted that he was not worthy to perform the most menial service for Him whose advent he announced. "I am content," he said in effect, "to be a voice, raised for a moment to proclaim the King, and soon dying on the desert air, while the person of the crier is unnoticed and unsought for; but I may not presume to unloose the latchet of His shoes. . . . There cometh after me He that is mightier than I, the latchet of whose shoes I am not worthy to stoop down and unloose.''

For thirty years the Son of Man had been about His Father's business in the ordinary routine of a village carpenter's life. He had found scope enough there for His marvelously rich and deep nature; reminding us of the philosopher's garden, which, though only a dingy court in a crowded city, reached through to the other side of the world on the one hand, and up to the haven of God on the other. Often He must have felt the strong attraction of the great world of men, which He loved; and the wild winds, as they careered over His village home, must have often borne to Him the wail of broken hearts, asking Him to hasten to their relief. On His ear must have struck the voices of Jairuses pleading for their only daughters; of sisters interceding for their Lazaruses; of halt and lame and blind entreating that He would come and heal them. But He waited still, His eye on the dial plate of the clock, till the time was fulfilled which had been fixed in the Eternal Council Chamber.

As soon, however, as the rumors of the Baptist's ministry reached Him, and He knew that the porter had taken up his position at the door of the sheepfold, ready to admit the true Shepherd (John 10:3), He could hesitate no longer. "Then cometh Jesus from Galilee to the Jordan unto John, to be baptized of him" (Matt. 3:13).

It may have been in the late afternoon when Jesus arrived. An expression made use of by the evangelist Luke might seem to suggest that all the people had been baptized for the day at least (Luke 3:21); so that perhaps the crowds had dispersed, and the great prophet was alone with one or two of those young disciples of whom we have spoken. Or, Jesus may have arrived when the Jordan banks were alive with the eager multitudes. But, in either case, a sudden and remarkable change passed over the Baptist's face as he beheld his Kinsman standing there.

Picture that remarkable scene. The arrowy stream, rushing down from the Lake of Galilee to the Dead Sea; the rugged banks; the shadowy forests; the erect, sinewy form of the Baptist; and Jesus of Nazareth, as depicted by the olden traditions, with auburn hair, searching blue eye, strong, sweet face, and all the beauty of His young manhood. At the sight of Him, note how the high look on the Baptist's face lowers; how his figure stoops in involuntary obeisance; how the voice that was wont to ring out its messages in accents of uncompromising decision falters and trembles!

John said, "I knew Him not" (John 1:31); but this need not be interpreted as indicating that he had no acquaintance whatever with his blameless relative. Such may have been the case, of course, since John's life had been spent apart from the haunts of men. It is more natural to suppose that the cousins had often met, as boys and afterwards. But the Baptist had never realized that Jesus was the Messiah whose advent he was sent to announce.

But John knew enough of Him to be aware of His guileless, blameless life. The story of His tender love for Mary; of His devotion to the interests of His brothers and sisters; of His undefiled purity; of His long vigils on the mountains till the morning called Him back to His toils; of His deep acquaintance with Scripture; of His speech about the Father—had reached the Baptist's ears. He had come to entertain the profoundest respect amounting to veneration for his Kinsman; and, as He presented Himself for baptism, John felt that there was a whole heaven of difference between Him and all others. These publicans and sinners, these Pharisees and scribes, these soldiers and common people—had every need to repent, confess, and be forgiven; but there was surely no such need for Him, who had been always, and by general acknowledgment, "holy, harmless, undefiled, and separate from sinners." "I have need," said he, "to be baptized of Thee, and comest Thou to me?" (Matt. 3:14).

There may have been, besides, an indescribable presentiment that stole over that lofty nature—like that knowledge of good men and bad which is often given to noble women. He knew men; his eagle eye had searched their hearts, as he had heard them confess their sins; and at a glance he could tell what was in them. A connoisseur of souls was he. It needed a Baptist to recognize the Christ. He who had never quailed before monarch or people, directly he came in contact with Christ, cast the crown of his manhood at his feet, and shrank away. The eagle that had soared unhindered in mid-heaven seemed transfixed by a sudden dart, and fell suddenly, with a strange, low cry, at the feet of its Creator. "I have need to be baptized of Thee, and comest Thou to me?" (Matt. 3:14).

"Suffer it to be so now; for thus it becometh us to fulfill all righteousness"—with such words our Lord overruled the objections of His loyal and faithful Forerunner. This is the first recorded utterance of Christ, after a silence of more than twenty years; the first also of His public ministry: it demands our passing notice.

In His baptism, our Lord acknowledged the divine authority of the Forerunner. As the last and greatest of the prophets, who was to close the Old Testament era, for "the law and the prophets prophesied until John"; as the representative of Elijah the prophet, before the great and notable day of the Lord could come; as the porter of the Jewish fold—John occupied a unique position, and it was out of deference to his office, that Jesus sought baptism at his hands.

John's baptism, moreover, was the inauguration of the Kingdom of Heaven. It was the outward and visible sign that Judaism was unavailing for the deepest needs of the spirit of man, and that a new and more spiritual system was about to take its place; and Christ said, in effect, "I, too, though King, obey the law of the Kingdom, and bow My head, that, by the same sign as the smallest of My subjects, I may pass forward to My throne."

There was probably a deeper reason still. His baptism was His formal identification with our fallen and sinful race, though He knew no sin Himself, and could challenge the minutest inspection of His enemies: "Which of you convinceth Me of sin?"

Was He baptized because He needed to repent, or to confess His sins? Nay, verily! He was as pure as the bosom of God, from which He came; as pure as the fire that shone above them in the orb of day; as pure as the snows on Mount Hermon, rearing itself like a vision of clouds on the horizon: but He needed to be made sin, that we might be made the righteousness of God in Him. When the paschal lamb had been chosen by the head of a Jewish household, it was customary to take it, three days before it would be offered, to the priest, to have it sealed with the Temple seal; so our Lord, three years before His death, must be set apart and sealed by the direct act of the Holy Spirit, through the mediation of John the Baptist. "Him hath God the Father sealed."

"It becometh us"—I like that word, *becometh*. If the Divine Lord thought so much about what was becoming, surely we may. It should not be a question with us, merely as to what may be forbidden or harmful, what may or may not be practiced and permitted by our fellow-Christians, or even whether there are distinct prohibitions in the Bible that bar the way—but if a certain course is becoming. "Need I pass through that rite?" *It is becoming.* "Need I perform that lowly act?" *It is becoming.* "Need I renounce my liberty of action in that respect?" *It would be very becoming.* And whenever some hesitant soul, timid and nervous to the last degree, dares to step out, and do what it believes to be the right thing because it is becoming, Jesus comes to it, enlinks his arm, and says, "Thou art not alone in this. Thou and I stand together here. It becomes *us* to fill up to its full measure all righteousness." Ah, soul, thou shalt never step forth on a difficult and untrodden path without hearing His footfall behind thee, and becoming aware that in every act of righteousness Christ identifies Himself, saying, "Thus it becometh *us* to fulfil all righteousness."

"Then he suffered Him." Some things we have to *do* for Christ, and some to *bear* for Him. Active virtues are great; but the passive ones are rare and cost more, especially for strong natures like the Baptist's. But, in all our human life, there is nothing more attractive than when a strong man yields to another, accepts a deeper interpretation of duty than he had perceived, and is prepared to set aside his strong convictions of propriety before the tender pleading of a still, soft voice. Yield to Christ, dear heart. Suffer Him to have His way. Take His yoke, and be meek and lowly of heart—so shalt thou find rest.

What a theophany was here! "I knew Him not" (i.e., as Son of God), "but He that sent me to baptize with water, He said unto me, 'Upon whomsoever thou shalt see the Spirit descending, and abiding upon Him, the same is He that baptizeth with the Holy Spirit.' And I have seen, and have borne witness that this is the Son of God" (John 1:32-34). "Lo, the heavens were opened unto him" (i.e., the Baptist), "and he saw the Spirit of God descending as a dove, and coming upon Him" (Matt. 3:16).

As the Man of Nazareth emerged from the water, the sign for which John had been eagerly waiting and looking was granted. He had believed he would see it, but had never thought to see it granted to one so near akin to himself. We never expect the great God to come to *us!* And the exclamation, *Lo,* indicates his startled surprise. He saw far away into the blue vault, which had opened into depth after depth of golden glory. The veil was rent to admit the coming forth of the Divine Spirit, who seemed to descend in visible shape—as a dove might, with gentle, fluttering motion—and to alight on the head of the Holy One, who stood there fresh from His baptism. The stress of the narrator, as he told the story afterwards, was that the Spirit not only came, but *abode.* Here was the miracle of miracles, that He should be willing to *abide* in any human temple, who for so many ages had wandered restlessly over the deluge of human sin, seeking a resting place, but finding none. Here, at least, was an ark into which this second Noah might pull in the fluttering dove, unable to feed, like the raven, on corruption and death.

The voice of God from heaven proclaimed that Jesus of

Nazareth was His beloved Son, in whom He was well pleased; and the Baptist could have no further doubt that the Desire of all Nations, the Lord whom His people sought, the Messenger of the Covenant, had suddenly come to His temple to act as a refiner's fire and as fuller's soap. "John bare witness saying, I have beheld the Spirit descending as a dove out of heaven; and it abode upon Him." "John beareth witness of Him and crieth" (John 1:15, 32).

He knew that his mission was nearly fulfilled, that his office was ended. He had opened the gate to the true Shepherd, and must now soon consign to Him all charge of the flock.

6

Not That Light, but a Witness

John 1:8

The baptism and revelation of Christ had a marvelous effect on the ministry of the Forerunner. Previous to that memorable day, the burden of his teaching had been in the direction of repentance and confession of sin. But afterwards, the whole force of his testimony was towards the person and glory of the Shepherd of Israel.

"The Jews sent unto him from Jerusalem priests and Levites to ask him, 'Who art thou?' . . . 'Why baptizest thou?' " (John 1:19, 25). The first question was universally interesting; the second specially so to the Pharisee party, who were the high ritualists of their day, and who were reluctant that a new rite, which they had not sanctioned, should be added to the Jewish ecclesiastical system.

It is a striking scene. The rushing river; the tropical gorge; the dense crowds of people standing thick together; the Baptist in his sinewy strength and uncouth attire, surrounded by the little group of disciples; while through the throng a deputation of greybeards, the representatives of a decadent religion, makes its difficult way—these are the principal features of a memorable incident.

There was a profound silence, and men craned their necks and strained their ears to see and hear everything, as the deputation challenged the prophet with the inquiry, "Who art thou?" There was a great silence. Men were prepared to believe anything of the eloquent young preacher: "The people were in expectation, and all men reasoned in their hearts concerning John, whether haply he were the Christ" (Luke 3:15). If he had given the least encouragement to their dreams and hopes, they would have unfurled again the tattered banner of the Maccabees; and beneath his leadership would have swept, like a wild hurricane, against the Roman occupation, gaining, perhaps, a momentary success, which afterwards would have been wiped out in blood. "And he confessed and denied not; and he confessed, I am not the Christ" (John 1:20).

If a murmur of voices burst out in anger, disappointment, and chagrin, as this answer spread from lip to lip, it was immediately hushed by the second inquiry propounded, "What then? Art thou Elijah?" (alluding to the prediction of Malachi 4:5). If they had worded their question rather differently, and put it thus, "Hast thou come in the power of Elias?" John must have acknowledged that it was so; but if they meant to inquire if he were literally Elijah returned again to this world, he had no alternative but to say, decisively and laconically "I am not."

There was a third arrow in their quiver, since the other two had missed the mark: and amid the deepening attention of the listening multitudes, and in allusion to Moses' prediction that God would raise up a Prophet like to himself (Deut. 18:15; Acts 3:22; 7:37), they said, "Art thou the Prophet?" and he answered, "No."

The deputation was nonplussed. They had exhausted their repertory of questions. Their mission threatened to become abortive, unless they could extract some positive admission. They must put a leading question; and their spokesman, for the fourth time, challenged the strange being, whom they found it so hard to label and place on any shelf of their ecclesiastical museum. "They said therefore unto him, 'Who art thou?—that we may give an answer to them that sent us.' What sayest thou of thyself?" "He said, 'I am the voice of one crying in the wilderness, Make straight the way of the Lord, as said Isaiah the prophet.' "

How infinitely noble! How characteristic of strength! When they complimented him on his teaching, he told them that He who would winnow the wheat from the chaff was yet to appear. And when they crowded to his baptism, he reiterated that it was only the baptism of negation, *of water*, but the Christ would baptize with the Holy Ghost and with fire.

Why was this? Ah, he knew his limitations! He was the greatest born of woman, yet he knew that his bosom was not broad enough, nor his heart tender enough, to justify him in bidding all weary and heavy laden ones to come to him for rest; he could not say that he and God were one, and include himself with the Deity, in the majestic pronoun, *we;* he never dared to ask men to believe in himself as they believed in the Father: but there came after him One who dared to say all these things.

Such humility always accompanies a true vision of Christ. "And they asked him, and said unto him, 'Why, then, baptizest thou, if thou art not the Christ, neither Elijah, neither the Prophet?' " (John 1:25). And John said in effect, "I baptize because I was sent to baptize, and I know very well that my work in this respect is temporary and transient; but what matters that? In the midst of you standeth One whom ye know not, even He that cometh after me, the latchet of whose shoe I am not worthy to unloose. The Christ is come. Have not I seen Him, standing amid your crowds, yea, descending these very banks?"

The people must have turned one to another, as he spoke. What! Had the Messiah come! It could hardly be. What is there to be seen that they cannot see? What heard that they cannot detect? Ah, "the natural man receiveth not the things of the Spirit of God, for they are foolishness unto him; neither can he know them, because they are spiritually discerned" (I Cor. 2:14). "There standeth One among you," said the Baptist, "whom ye know not" (John 1:26).

Six weeks passed by from that memorable vision of the opened heaven and the descending Spirit, and John had eagerly scanned every comer to the river bank to see again that divinely beautiful face. But in vain: for Jesus was in the wilderness, being tempted of the devil, for forty days and nights, the companion of wild beasts, exposed to a hurricane of temptation.

At the end of the six weeks, the interview with the deputation from the Sanhedrin took place, which we have already described; and on the day after, when his confession of inferiority was still fresh in the minds of his hearers, when some were criticizing and others pitying, when symptoms that the autumn of his influence had set in were in the air, his eyes flashed, his face lit up, and he cried, saying: "This is He of whom I said, 'After me cometh a man who is become before me, for He was before me.' Behold the Lamb of God, which taketh away the sin of the world" (John 1:29, 30).

Did all eyes turn towards the Christ? Was there a ripple of interest and expectancy through the crowd? We know not. Scripture is silent, only telling us that on the following day, when, with two disciples, he looked on Jesus as He walked, and repeated his affirmation, "Behold the Lamb of God," those two disciples followed Him, never to return to their old master—who knew it must be so and was content to decrease if only *He* might increase.

Let us notice the successive revelations which were made to John, and through him to Israel.

Christ's Pre-existence

"He was before me" (John 1:30). The phrase resembles Christ's own words, when He said: "Before Abraham was, I am." In John's case it developed soon after into another and kindred expression: "He that cometh from above, is above all" (John 3:31). With such words the Baptist taught his disciples. He insisted that Jesus of Nazareth had an existence anterior to Nazareth, and previous to His birth of the village maiden. He recognized that His goings had been of old, even from everlasting, that He was the mighty God, the Father of the Ages, and the Prince of Peace. As for himself, he was of the earth, and of the earth he spoke; as for this One, He came from above, and was above all. It is not surprising, therefore, that one of his disciples, catching his Master's spirit, wrote: "In the beginning was the Word, and the Word was with God, and the Word was God. The same was in the beginning with God. All things were made by Him."

The Sacrificial Aspect of Christ's Work

"Behold the Lamb of God, which taketh away the sin of the world." An attempt has been made to limit the meaning of these words to the personal character of Jesus, His purity, and gentleness; but, to the Jews who listened, the latter part of his exclamation could have but one significance. They would at once connect with his words, those of the Law, the Prophets, and the Psalms. "The goat shall bear upon him all their iniquities unto a solitary land." "He bare the sin of many." "He is led as a lamb to the slaughter" (Isaiah 53:12, 7).

From the slopes of Mount Moriah, a young voice has expressed the longing of the ages, "Behold the fire and the wood; but where is the lamb?" "Every priest," is the comment of inspiration, "standeth day by day ministering and offering oftentimes the same sacrifices, the which can never take away sins" (Heb. 10:11). Animals at the best are only symbols of the complete solution to the ever-recurring problem of human sin. Then from His heaven God sends forth His Son to be the sufficient answer to the universal appeal: and the heaven-sent messenger, from his rocky pulpit, as he sees Jesus coming to him, cries, "Behold the Lamb of God, which taketh away the sin of the world."

Dear soul, thou mayest venture on Him. He is God's Lamb; on Him the sin of our race has been laid, and He stood before God with the accumulated load—"made sin"; the iniquity of us all was laid upon Him; wounded for our transgressions; bruised for our iniquities; chastised for our peace; striken for our transgression; bearing the sin of many. As the first Adam brought sin on the race, the second Adam has put it away by the sacrifice of Himself. Men are lost now, not because of Adam's sin, nor because they were born into a race of sinners, but for the sin which they presumptuously and wilfully commit, or because by unbelief they contract themselves out of the benefits of Christ's death.

The Baptism of the Holy Spirit
"The same is He that baptizeth with the Holy Spirit" (John 1:33). As Son of God, our Savior from all eternity was one with the Holy Spirit in the mystery of the blessed Trinity; but as "the one Man," He received in His human nature the fulness of the Divine Spirit. It pleased the Father that in Him should all the fulness of the Godhead dwell, that He might be able to communicate Him to all the sons of men who were united to Him by a living faith. Thus it fell that He was able to assure His disciples that if they waited in Jerusalem for the promise of the Father, as John baptized with water, they should be baptized with the Holy Spirit (Acts 1:4, 5).

The Mystery of the Holy Trinity
For the first time this was made manifest to man. On the one hand there was the Father speaking from heaven; on the other the Spirit descending as a dove—and between them was the Son of Man who was proclaimed to be the Son of God, the beloved Son. Surely John might say that flesh and blood had not revealed these things, but they had come by a divine revelation.

The doctrine of the Holy Trinity is a profound mystery, hidden from the intellect, but revealed to the humble and reverent heart; hidden from the wise and prudent, and revealed to babes. Welcome Jesus Christ as John did; and, as to John, so the whole wonder of the Godhead will be made known to thy heart. Thou wilt hear the Father bearing witness to His Son; thou wilt see how clearly the Son reveals the Father, and achieves redemption; thou shalt know what it is to stand beneath the open heaven and behold and participate in the Divine anointing. Of what good is it to reason about the Trinity if thou has no spiritual appetite for the gifts of the

Trinity? But if this is thine, and thou openest thine heart, thou wilt receive the gift and understand the doctrine.

The Divine Sonship of Christ

"I have seen and have borne witness that this is the Son of God" (John 1:34). This witness counts for much. John knew men, knew himself, knew Christ. He would not have said so much unless he had been profoundly convinced; and he would not have been profoundly convinced unless irrefragable evidence has been presented to him. What though, when on the following day he repeats his exclamation, his whole congregation leaves him to follow the Man of Nazareth to His home? The heart of the Forerunner is satisfied, for he has heard the Bridegroom's voice. The Son of God has come, and has given him an understanding that he might know Him that is true.

7

He Must Increase,
but I Must Decrease

John 3:30

From the Jordan Valley our Lord returned to Galilee and
Nazareth. The marriage feast of Cana, His return to Jerusalem, the cleansing of the Temple, and the interview with
Nicodemus, followed in rapid succession. And when the
crowds of Passover pilgrims were dispersing homewards, He
also left the city with His disciples, and began a missionary
tour throughout the land of Judea.

This tour is not much dwelt upon in Scripture.

Of the commencement of His ministry it is recorded:
"Jesus came, . . . preaching the Gospel of God, and saying,
'The time is fulfilled, and the Kingdom of God is at hand:
repent ye, and believe the Gospel' " (Mark 1:14, 15). But His
deeds declared His royalty.

Wherever He went He was welcomed with vast enthusiasm.

During all this time the Baptist was continuing his preparatory work in the Jordan Valley, though now driven by
persecution to leave the western bank for Aenon and Salim
on the eastern side, where a handful of followers still clung to
him. "John was not yet cast into prison," but the shadow of
his impending fate was already gathering over him.

It would appear from the Revised Version (v. 25) that a
Jew, probably an emissary of the Sanhedrin, brought tidings

to that little circle of true-hearted disciples of the work that Jesus was doing in Judea, and drew them into a discussion as to the comparative value of the two baptisms. The Baptist's disciples came to him with eyes flashing with indignation, and faces heated with the excitement of the discussion: "Rabbi, He that was with thee beyond Jordan, to whom thou hast borne witness, the same baptizeth, and all men come to Him" (v. 26).

It was as though they said, "Master, is it not too bad? See how thy generous testimony has been requited! In the day of thy glory thou wert too profuse in thy acknowledgments, too prodigal in thy testimonials. Now this new Teacher has taken a leaf out of thy program; He too is preaching, baptizing, and gathering a school of disciples." But there was no tinder in that noble breast which these jealous sparks could kindle. Nothing but love dwelt there. Thus his reply will ever rank among the greatest utterances of mortal man. The Lord said that of those born of woman none was greater than John; and if by nothing else, by these words his moral stature and superlative excellence were vindicated. He seemed great when his voice rang like a clarion through Palestine, attracting and thrilling the mighty throngs; great, when he dared to tell Herod that it was unlawful for him to have his brother's wife, uttering words which those palace walls must have been startled to hear; great, when he baptized Him for whom the world was waiting, and who was declared to be the Son of God with power: but he never seemed so great as when he refused to enter into those acrimonious altercations and discussions, and said simply, "A man can receive nothing, except it be given him from heaven" (John 3:27).

This is a golden sentence, indeed!—"A man can receive nothing, except it be given him from heaven." Hast thou great success in thy lifework? Do crowds gather around thy steps and throng thy audience chamber? Do not attribute them to thyself. They are all the gifts of God's grace. He raiseth up one and setteth down another. Thou hast nothing that thou hast not received; and if thou hast received it, see to it that thou exercise perpetually the faculty of receptiveness, so that thou mayest receive more and more, grace on grace. The river in its flow should hollow out the channelbed through which it flows. Be thankful, but never vain. He who gave may take. Great talents bestowed imply great responsibility in the day of reckoning. Be not arrogant, but fear. Much success can only be enjoyed without injury to the inner life by being considered as the dear gift of Christ, to be used for Him.

Hast thou but one talent, and little success?—yet this is as God has willed it. He might have given more had He willed it so; be thankful that He has given any. Use what thou hast. The five barley loaves and two small fishes will so increase, as they are distributed, that they will supply the want of thousands. Do not dare to envy one more successful and used than thyself, lest thou be convicted of murmuring against the appointment of thy Lord.

Here, too, is the cure of jealousy, which more than anything else blights the soul of the servant of God. God has meant each of us for something; incarnating in us one of His own great thoughts, and equipping us with all material that is necessary for its realization. Every name is historic in God's estimate. The obscurest among us has his place in the Divine plan, his lesson to learn, his work to do. The century opening before us can no more dispense with us than an orchestra with the piccolo. "We are His workmanship, created in Christ Jesus unto good works which God has before prepared, that we should walk in them" (Eph. 2:10).

The Messiah opens His ministry among men by mingling with the simple villagers in their wedding joy, and actually ministers to their innocent mirth, as He turns the water into wine! The Son of Man has come "eating and drinking"! What a contrast was here to the austerity of the desert, the coarse raiment, the hard fare! "John the Baptist came neither eating nor drinking." Could this be He? And yet there was no doubt that the heaven had been opened above Him, that the Dove had descended, and that God's voice had declared Him to be the "Beloved Son." But what a contrast to all that he had looked for!

Further reflection, however, on that incident, in which Jesus manifested forth His glory and the cleansing of the Temple which immediately followed, must have convinced the Baptist that this conception of holiness was the true one. His own type could never be universal or popular. It was not to be expected that the mass of men could be spared from the ordinary demands of daily life to spend their days in the wilderness as he had done; and it would not have been for their well-being, or that of the world, if his practice had become the rule. It would have been a practical admission that ordinary life was common and unclean; and that there was no possibility of infusing it with the high principles of the Kingdom of Heaven. Consecration to God would have become synonymous with the exclusion of wife and child, of home and business, of music and poetry, from the soul of the saint; whereas its true conception demands that nothing which God has created can be accounted common or unclean, but all may be included within the encircling precincts of the Redeemer's Kingdom. The motto of Christian consecration is, therefore, given in that remarkable assertion of the apostle: "Every creature of God is good, and nothing is to be rejected, if it be received with thanksgiving: for it is sanctified through the Word of God and prayer" (1 Tim. 4:4, 5).

John saw, beneath the illuminating ray of the Holy Spirit, that this was the Divine Ideal; that the Redeemer could not contradict the Creator; that the Kingdom was consistent with the home; and the presence of the King with the caress of woman and the laughter of the child, and the innocent mirth of the village feast. This he saw, and cried in effect: "That village scene is the key to the Messiah's ministry to Israel. He is not only Guest at a bridegroom's table, but the Bridegroom Himself. He has come to woo and win the chosen race. Of old they were called Hephzibah and Beulah; and now those ancient words come back to mind with newly minted meaning, with the scent of spring. Our land, long bereaved and desolate, is to be married. Joy, joy to her! The bridegroom is here. He that hath the bride is the Bridegroom. As for me, I am the Bridegroom's friend, sent to negotiate the match, privileged to know and bring together the two parties in the blessed nuptials—blessed with the unspeakable gladness of hearing the Bridegroom's manly speech. Do you tell me that He is preaching, and that all come to Him? That is what I have wanted most of all. This my joy, therefore, is fulfilled. 'He must increase, but I must decrease.' "

Consider, then, the Baptist's creed at this point of his career. He *believed* in the heavenly origin and divinity of the Son of Man—that He was from heaven and above all. He *believed* in the unique and divine source of His teaching—that He did not communicate what He had learned second-hand, but stood forth as one speaking what He knows, and testifying what He has seen—"For He whom God has sent, speaketh the words of God." He *believed* in His copious enduement with the Holy Spirit. Knowing that human teachers, at the best, could only receive the Spirit in a limited degree, he recognized that when God anointed Jesus of Nazareth with the Holy Spirit there was no limit, no measuring meter, no stint. It was copious, rich, unmeasured—so much so that it ran down from His head, as Hermon's dews descended to the lonely heights of Zion. He *believed* in His near relationship to God, using the well-known Jewish phrase of sonship to describe His possession of the divine nature in a unique sense, and recalling the utterance of the hour of baptism, to give weight to his assurance that the Father loved Him as Son. Lastly, he *believed* in the mediatorial function of the Man of Nazareth—that the Father had already given all things into His hand; and that the day was coming when He would sit on the throne of David, yea, on the mediatorial throne itself, King of kings, and Lord of lords, the keys of Death and Hades, of the realms of invisible existence and spiritual power, hanging at His girdle.

To that creed the Baptist added a testimony, which has

been the means of light and blessing to myriads. Being dead, he yet has spoken through the ages, assuring us that to believe on Jesus is to have, as a present fact, eternal life, the life which fills the Being of God and defies time and change. Faith is the act by which we open our heart to receive the gift of God; as earth bares her breast to sun and rain, and as the good wife flings wide her doors and windows to let in the spring sunshine and the summer air. Ah, reader, I would that thou hadst this faith! The open heart towards Christ! The yielded will! Thou needst only will to have Him, and He has already entered though thou canst not detect His footfall, or the chime of the bells around His garment's hem. And to shut thy heart against Him not only excludes the life which might be thine, but incurs the wrath of God. The only hope of a decreasing self is an increasing Christ. There is too much of the self life in us all.

The Son of God is not content to love us. He cannot rest till He has all our love in return. "He looketh in at the windows" of the soul, "and showeth Himself through the lattice." Our Beloved speaks, and says unto us, "Rise up, my love, my fair one, and come away."

8
The King's Courts
Mark 6

Our story brings us next to speak of the Baptist's relations with Herod Antipas. From an early age he had been entrusted with despotic power, and, as the natural and inevitable result, had become sensual, weak, capricious, and cruel.

It is of the collision between this man, whom our Lord compared to a fox, and John the Baptist, that we have now to treat. We need only notice here that every great character on the page of history has had his vehement antagonist. Moses, Pharaoh; Elijah, Ahab; Jeremiah, Jehoiakim; Paul, Nero; Savonarola, the Medici; Luther, the Emperor Charles V.

All the world had flocked to see and hear John the Baptist. Every mouth was full of his eccentricities and eloquence. All this was well known to Herod. His spies were present in every great gathering, and served the purpose of the newspapers of today; so that he was well informed of all the topics that engaged the popular mind.

For some months, also, Herod had watched the career of the preacher. When he least expected it, he was under the surveillance of the closest criticism. And the result had been perfectly satisfactory. Herod felt that John was a true man. He observed him, and was satisfied that he was a just man and a holy. Reasons of state forbade the king from going in person to the Jordan Valley; but he was extremely eager to see and hear this mighty man of God: and so, one day, at the close of a discourse, an argument with Pharisees, or the administration of the rite of baptism, John found himself accosted by one of the court chamberlains, and summoned to deliver his message before the court. Herod "sent for him."

We might wonder how it could happen that a man like Herod should be so willing to call in so merciless a preacher of repentance as John the Baptist was. But it must be remembered that most men, when they enter the precincts of the court, are accustomed to put velvet in their mouths; and, however vehement they may have been in denouncing the sins of the lower classes, they change their tone when face to face with sinners in high places. Herod, therefore, had every reason to presume that John would obey this unwritten law; and while denouncing sin in general, would refrain from anything direct and personal.

One interpretation of Mark 6:20 suggests that the Baptist's first sermon before Herod was followed by another, and yet another. We are told that he used to hear *(the imperfect tense)* him gladly, and "did many things." It was a relief to Herod's mind to feel that there were many things which he could do, many wrongs which he could set right, while the main wrong of his life was left untouched. Ah! it is remarkable how much men will do in the direction of amendment and reform, if only, by a tacit understanding, nothing is said, or hinted at, which threatens the one sin in which the heart's evil has contented itself. But—John knew that his duty to Herod, to truth, to public morality, demanded that he should go further, and pierce to the dividing asunder of soul and spirit, of the joints and marrow; and therefore on one memorable occasion he accosted the royal criminal with the crime of which men were speaking secretly everywhere, and uttered the sentence which could not be forgiven: "It is not lawful for thee to have thy brother's wife" (v. 18).

The sermon began. As was John's wont, he arraigned the sin, the formalism, the laxity of the times; he proclaimed the advent of the Kingdom, the presence of the King; he demanded, in the name of God, repentance and reform. Herod was, as usual, impressed and convinced; he assented to the preacher's propositions; already he had settled himself into his usual posture for hearing gladly. It was as when we watch summer lightning playing around the horizon; we have no fear so long as it is not forked.

Presently, however, John becomes more personal and direct than ever before. He begins, in no measured terms, to denounce the sin of men in high places, and holds up the dissoluteness which disgraced the court. As he proceeds, a breathless silence falls on the crowd sitting, or hanging around him, their dresses in curious contrast to his severe garment of camel's hair; their nervous dread in as great contrast to his incisive and searching eloquence. Here were the people clothed in soft raiment, and accustomed to sumptuous fare, bending as reeds before the gusts of wind sweeping fiercely across the marsh.

Finally, the preacher comes closer still, and pointing to the princess who sat beside Herod, looking Herod in the face, he exclaims: "It is not lawful for thee to have thy brother's wife."

We need not dwell on all the terrible details of that disgraceful sin. But every circumstance which could deepen its infamy was present. Herod's wife, the daughter of Aretas, King of Arabia, was still living; as was Philip, the husband of Herodias. The liaison commenced at Rome, when Herod was the guest of his brother Philip, while apparently engaged on a mission of holy devotion to the religious interests of the Jewish nation.

The ground of John's accusation calls for a heavier emphasis than appears in a superficial consideration of the words. He might have said: "It is not expedient; your wife's father will rise in arms against you, and threaten the Eastern border of your kingdom. It is not expedient to run the risk of war, which may give Rome a further excuse against you." He might have said: "This is an unwise step, as it will cut you off from your own family, and leave you exposed to the brunt of popular hate." He might have said: "It is impolitic and incautious to risk the adverse judgment of the Emperor." But he said none of these things. He took the matter to a higher court. He arraigned the guilty pair before God; and, laying his axe at the root of the tree—calling on Herod's conscience, long gagged and silent, to take part in the impeachment—he said, in effect: "I summon you before the bar of God, and in the pure light which streams from His holy Oracle, your consciences being witness against you, you know perfectly well that it is not right for you to be living as you are living. 'Thou shalt not commit adultery.' "

Every hearer stood aghast. A deathlike hush fell on the assembly, which probably broke up in dismay. So paralyzed was every one that no hand was laid on the preacher. We are expressly told that "Herod *sent forth* and laid hold upon John" (Mark 6:17); from which we infer that the fearless preacher passed out through the paralyzed and conscience-striken assemblage, leaving dismay, like that which befell the roysterers in Belshazzar's court, when the hand of the Almighty traced the mysterious characters on the palace walls in lines of fire.

The first feeling of awe and conscience-striken remorse would, however, soon pass off. Some would hasten to condole with Herodias; some to sympathize with Herod. Herodias would retire to her apartments, accompanied by her high ladies, vowing fiery vengeance on the preacher—a very Jezebel, thirsting for the blood of another Elijah. Throughout Herod's court there would be an effort to dismiss the allusion as "Altogether uncalled for," as "What might have been expected from such a man."

But Herodias would give her paramour no rest; and, perhaps one evening, when John had retired for meditation and prayer, his disciples being off their guard and the people absent, a handful of soldiers arrested him, bound him, and led him off to the strong castle of Macherus.

From time to time it would seem as though the strictness of John's imprisonment was relaxed. His disciples were permitted to see him, and tell him of what was happening in the world without; but stranger than all, he was summoned to have audiences with Herod himself.

First, he was deeply incensed. As he thought of the manner in which the Baptist had treated him, denouncing him before his court, the fire of anger burnt fiercely within his breast; and he had beside him a Lady Macbeth, a beautiful fiend and temptress, who knew that while the Baptist lived, and dared to speak as he had done, her position was not safe. She knew Herod well enough to dread the uprising of his conscience at the appeals of truth. And perpetually, when she saw her chance, she whispered in Herod's ear, "The sooner you do away with that man the better. You don't love me perfectly, as long as you permit him to breathe. Unmannerly cur!" "Herodias set herself against him, and desired to kill him; but she could not" (v. 19).

On the other side, Herod was in fear. He feared John, "knowing that he was a righteous man and a holy." He feared the people, because they held him for a prophet. And, beneath all, he feared God, lest He should step in to avenge any wrong perpetrated against His servant.

Between these two influences he was "much perplexed" (Mark 6:20). When he was with Herodias, he thought as she did, and left her, almost resolved to give the fatal order; but when he was alone, the other influence made itself felt, and he would send for John.

Well might the Lord ask, in after days, if John were a reed shaken with the wind. Rather he resembled a forest tree, whose deeply struck and far-spreading roots secure it against the attack of the hurricane; or a mighty Alp, which defies the tremor of the earthquake, and rears its head above the thunderstorms, which break upon its slopes, to hold fellowship with the skies.

Again and again John was remanded to his cell. Probably twelve months passed thus. The story does not end here. He not only murdered John the Baptist, but he inflicted a deadly wound on his own moral nature, from which it never recovered.

9
Art Thou He?

Matthew 11

It is very touching to remark the tenacity with which some few of John's disciples clung to their great leader. They could not forget what he had been to them—that he had first called them to the reality of living; that he had taught them to pray; that he had led them to the Christ. To be loved like that is earth's deepest bliss!

They did not hesitate to come to his cell with tidings of the great outer world, and specially of what *He* was doing and saying, whose life was so mysteriously bound up with his own. "The disciples of John told him of all these things" (Luke 7:18).

It was to two of these choice and steadfast friends that John confided the question which had long been forming within his soul, and forcing itself to the front. "And John, calling unto him two of his disciples, sent them to the Lord, saying, Art Thou He that cometh, or look we for another?" (Luke 7:19).

The Bible does not scruple to tell us of the failures of its noblest children. And in this the Spirit of God has rendered us untold service, because we learn that the material out of which He made the greatest saints was flesh and blood like ourselves; and that it was by divine grace, manifested very conspicuously towards them, that they became what they were. *He sent them to Jesus, saying, Art Thou He that should come?* We can easily trace this lapse of faith to three sources.

Depression. We are all so highly strung, so delicately balanced. Often the lack of spiritual joy and peace and power in prayer is attributable to nothing else than our confinement in the narrow limits of a tiny room; to the foul, gaseous air we are compelled to breathe; to our inability to get beyond the great city, with its wilderness of brick, into the country, with its blossoms, fields, and woodland glades. In a large number of spiritual maladies the physician is more necessary than the minister of religion; a holiday by the seaside or on the mountains, than a convention.

What an infinite comfort it is to be told that God knows how easily our nature may become jangled and out of tune. He can attribute our doubts and fears to their right source. He knows the bow is bent to the point of breaking, and the string strained to its utmost tension. He does not rebuke His servants when they cast themselves under juniper bushes, and ask to die; but sends them food and sleep. And when they send from their prisons, saying, Art Thou He? there is no word of rebuke, but of tender encouragement and instruction.

Disappointment. When first consigned to prison, he had expected every day that Jesus would in some way deliver him. We can sympathize in this also. With ears alert, and our heart throbbing with expectancy, we have lain in our prison cell listening for the first faint footfall of the angel; but the weary hours have passed without bringing him, and we have questioned whether God were mindful of His own; whether prayer prevailed; whether the promises were to be appropriated by *us?*

Partial views of Christ. "John heard in the prison the works of Jesus" (Matt. 11:2). They were wholly beneficent and gentle. "He has laid His hands on a few sick folk, and healed them; has gathered a number of children to His arms, and blessed them; has sat on the mountain, and spoken of rest and peace and blessedness."

"Is that all? Has He not used the fan to winnow the wheat, and the fire to burn up the chaff? I cannot understand it. This quiet gentle life of benevolence is outside my calculations. There must be some mistake. Go and ask Him whether we should expect *another*, made in a different mold, and who shall be as the fire, the earthquake, the tempest, while He is as the still small voice."

John had partial views of the Christ—he thought of Him only as the Avenger of sin, the Maker of revolution, the dread Judge of all. There was apparently no room in his conception of the gentler, sweeter, tenderer aspect of his Master's nature. And for want of a clearer understanding of what God by the mouth of His holy prophets had spoken since the world began, he fell into this Slough of Despond.

It was a grievous pity; yet let us not blame him too vehemently, lest we blame ourselves. We think, for instance, that if there be a righteous God, He will not permit wrong to triumph; little children to suffer for the sins of their parents; the innocent to be trodden beneath the foot of the oppressor and the proud; or the dumb creatures to be tortured in the supposed interest of medical science. Surely God will step out of His hiding place and open all prisons, emancipate all captives, and wave a hand of benediction over all creation. Thus we think and say; and then, because the world still groans and travails, we question whether God is in His high heaven.

The Lord's Indirect Reply
He did not say, I am He that was to come, do not look for another. Had He done so, He might have answered John's intellect, but not his heart. After a few hours the assurance would have waxed dim, and he would have questioned again. He might have wondered whether Jesus were not Himself deceived. One question always leads to another, so long as the heart is unsatisfied; hence the refusal on the part of our Lord to answer the question, and His evident determination to allay the restless and disquietude of the heart that throbbed beneath.

A Mysterious Answer

Surely, if He were able to do so much, He could do more. The power that healed the sick and lame and blind, and cast out demons, could surely deliver John. It made his heart the more wistful, to hear of these displays of power. He had to learn that the Lord healed these poor folks so easily because the light soil of their nature could not bear the richer harvests. It was because John was a royal soul, the greatest of woman born, because his nature was capable of yielding the best results to the divine culture, that he was kept waiting, while others caught up the blessing and went away healed. Only three months remained of life, and in these the discipline of patience and doubt must do their work.

That is where you have made a mistake. You have thought God was hard on you, that He would help everybody but you; but you have not understood that your nature was so dear to God, and so precious in His sight, and so capable of the greatest development, that God loved you too much to let you off so lightly, and give you what you wanted, and send you on your way. God could have given you sight, made that lame foot well, restored the child to health, and opened the iron prison door of your circumstances. *He could*; but for all eternity you will thank Him He did not, because you are capable of something else. We are kept waiting through the long years—not that He loves us less, but more; not that He refuses what we ask, but that in the long strain and tension He is making us partakers of His blessedness. John's nature would presently yield a martyr and win a martyr's crown: was not that reason enough for not giving him at once the deliverance he sought?

The Answer was Sufficient. Together with the works of beneficence, the Lord drew John's attention to words he seemed in danger of forgetting: "Strengthen ye the weak hands, and confirm the feeble knees. Say to them that are of a fearful heart, Be strong; fear not! Behold, your God will come with vengeance, with the recompense of God. He will come and save you. Then the eyes of the blind shall be opened;

and the ears of the deaf shall be unstopped; then shall the lame man leap as an hart, and the tongue of the dumb shall sing; for in the wilderness shall waters break out, and streams in the desert." "The Spirit of the Lord God is upon Me, because the Lord hath anointed Me to preach good tidings unto the meek; He hath sent Me to bind up the brokenhearted, to proclaim liberty to the captives, and the opening of the prison to them that are bound" (Isaiah 61:1). The Lord strove to convince the questioner that his views were too partial and limited, and to send him back to a more comprehensive study of the old Scriptures. It was as though Jesus said, "Go to your master, and tell him to take again the ancient prophecy and study it. He has taken the sterner predictions to the neglect of the gentler, softer ones. It is true that I am to proclaim the day of vengeance; but first I must reveal the acceptable year. It is true that I am to come as a Mighty One and My arm shall rule for Me; but it is also true that I am to feed My flock like a Shepherd, and gather the lambs in My arm."

A New Beatitude. "Blessed is he, whosoever shall not be offended in Me." Our Lord put within the reach of His noble Forerunner the blessedness of those who have not seen and yet have believed; of those who trust though they are slain; of those who wait the Lord's leisure; and of those who cannot understand His dealings, but rest in what they know of His heart. This is the beatitude of the unoffended, of those who do not stumble over the mystery of God's dealings with their life.

God's children are sometimes the most bitterly tried. For them the fires are heated seven times; days of weariness and nights of pain are appointed them; they suffer, not only at the hand of man, but it seems as though God Himself were turned against them, to become their enemy. The heavens seem as brass to their cries and tears, and the enemy has reason to challenge them with the taunt, "Where is now your God!" The waters of a full cup are wrung out in days like these; and the cry is extorted, "How long, O Lord, how long?"

You and I have been in this plight. We have said, "Hath God forgotten to be gracious? Has He in anger shut up His tender mercies?" If we will quiet our souls, light will break in on us as from the eternal morning; the peace of God will keep our hearts and minds, and we shall enter on the blessedness which our Lord unfolded before His faithful Forerunner.

10

None Greater Than
John the Baptist, Yet...

Matthew 11

While John's disciples were standing there, our Lord said nothing in his praise; but as soon as they had departed, the floodgates of His heart were thrown wide open, and He began to speak to the multitudes concerning His faithful servant. We say our kind things before each other's faces; our hard things when the back is turned. It is not so with Christ. Christ may never tell you how greatly He loves and values you; but while you lie there in your prison, with sad and overcast heart, He is saying and thinking great things about you yonder.

"Among them that are born of women, there hath not risen a greater than John the Baptist."

"But, dost Thou really mean, most holy Lord, that this one is the greatest born of woman?"

"Certainly," saith Christ, in effect.

"But he has asked if Thou art really the Messiah."

"I know it," saith the Lord.

"But how canst Thou say that he is to be compared with Moses, Isaiah, or Daniel? Did they doubt Thee thus? And how canst Thou say that he is not a reed shaken with the wind, when, but now, he gave patent evidence that he was stooping beneath the hurrying tread of gales of doubt and depression?"

"Ah," the Master seems to say, "Heaven judges, not by a passing mood, but by the general tenor and trend of a man's life; not by the expression of a doubt, caused by accidents which may be explained, but by the soul of man within him, which is as much deeper than the emotions as the heart of the ocean is deeper than the cloud shadows which hurry across its surface."

Yes, the Lord judges us by that which is deepest, most permanent, most constant and prevalent with us; by the ideal we seek to apprehend; by the decision and choice of our soul; by that bud of possibility which lies as yet furled, and unrealized even by ourselves.

Our Lord drew attention to three outstanding features of John's Character and Ministry.

His Independence. "What went ye out into the wilderness to behold? A reed shaken with the wind?" (Matt. 11:7). The language of the Bible is so picturesque, so full of natural imagery, that it appeals to every age, and speaks in every language of the world. Who on a gusty March day, has not watched the wind blowing lustily across a marsh or the reedy margin of a lake, compelling all the reeds to stoop in the same direction?

You, my reader, admire, but feel you cannot follow. When your companions and friends are speaking depreciating and ungenerous words of some public man whom you love; when unkind and scandalous stories are being passed from lip to lip; when a storm of execration and hatred is being poured on a cause, which in your heart you favor and espouse—you find it easier to bow before the gale, with all the other reeds around you, than to enter your protest, even though you stand alone. Yet the reed thrust by the soldiers into the hands of Christ may become the rod of iron with which He rules the nations. He can take the most pliant and yielding natures, and make them, as He made Jeremiah, "a defensed city, and an iron pillar, and brazen walls, against the whole land."

His simplicity. A second time the Master asked the people

what they went forth into the wilderness to behold; and by His question implied that John was no Sybarite clothed in soft raiment, and feasting in luxury, but a strong, pure soul, that had learned the secret of self-denial and self-control.

To all my young brothers and sisters who may read this page, and who have yet the making of their lives in their own hands, I would say, with all my heart, learn to do without the soft clothing and the many servants which characterize king's courts. At the table have your eye on the simpler dishes, those which supply the maximum of nutriment and strength, and do not allow your choice to be determined by what pleases the palate or gratifies the taste.

So with dress. Our Master does not require of us to dress grotesquely, or to attract notice by the singularity and grotesqueness of our attire. We must dress suitably and in conformity with that station in life to which He has called us. But what a difference there is between making our dress our main consideration, and considering first and foremost the attire of the soul in meekness and truth, purity and unselfishness. They who are set upon these may be trusted to put the other in the right place. But, on the whole, the truly consecrated soul should study simplicity. It should not endeavor to attract notice by glaring colors or extravagant display. It ought not to seek a large variety of dresses and costumes, but be satisfied with what may be really needed for the exigencies of climate and health. Let it take no pleasure in vying with others, because dress is a question of utility and not of pride.

So with service. We should know how to do everything for ourselves, and be prepared to do it whenever it is necessary. Of course, with some of us, it is essential that we should have help; that we may be set free to do the special work of our lives. Nothing would be more unfortunate than that those who are highly gifted in some special direction should fritter away their time and strength in doing trifles which others could do for them equally well.

His noble office. "But wherefore went ye out?—to see a

prophet? Yea, I say unto you, and much more than a prophet" (Matt. 11:9). Nothing is more difficult than to measure men while they are living. While the fascination of their presence and the music of their voice are in the air, we are apt to exaggerate their worth.

But our Lord went further, and did not hesitate to class John with the greatest of those born of women. He may have had peers, but no superiors; equals, but no over-lords. Who may be classed with him, we cannot, dare not, say. But probably Abraham, Moses, Paul. "There hath not arisen a greater than John the Baptist."

Our Lord went beyond John's own modest, self-depreciating estimate, and declared, "If ye are willing to receive it, this is Elijah which is to come." As He descended from the Mount of Transfiguration, He returned to the same subject: "And they asked Him, saying, The scribes say that Elijah must first come. And He said unto them, Elijah indeed cometh first, and restoreth all things. . . . But I say unto you that Elijah is come, and they have also done unto him whatsoever they listed, even as it is written of him" (Mark 9:9-13).

The Master's Reservation. Let us again quote His memorable words: "Among them that are born of women there hath not arisen a greater than John the Baptist; yet, he that is but little in the Kingdom of heaven is greater than he" (Matt. 11:11). It is always a sign of the greatest knowledge, when its possessor confesses himself to be a child picking up shells on the shores of a boundless ocean. And the Baptist's greatness was revealed in the lowliness of his self-estimate.

The greatness of John was proved in this that like his Lord he was meek and lowly in heart. Neither before nor since has a son of Adam lived in whom these divine qualities were more evident. No sublimer, no more God-like utterance ever passed the lips of man than John's answer to his disciples: "A man can receive nothing except it have been given him from heaven. He must increase, but I must decrease" (see the whole passage, John 3:27-36). The very same spirit of meekness was speaking in John as acted in his Lord, when knowing that the Pharisees had heard that Jesus was making and baptizing more disciples than John (though Jesus Himself baptized not, but His disciples), "He left Judea and departed into Galilee." What divisions might have been avoided in the Church had His people followed His example!

But what was in our Lord's thought when He made the reservation, *"Yet he that is but little in the Kingdom of Heaven is greater than he"*? It has been suggested that the Lord was speaking of John not only as a man, but as a prophet, and that this declaration applies more particularly to John as a prophet. The words of the evangelist Luke are noticeable— "There hath not risen a greater prophet than John the Baptist": because to balance the sentence it seems needful to supply the word *prophet* in the second clause—"The least prophet in the Kingdom of Heaven is a greater prophet than he." John could say, "Behold the Lamb of God"; but the least of those who, being scattered abroad, went everywhere proclaiming the word of the Kingdom, preached "Jesus and the resurrection."

And may there not be even more than this? The character of John was strong, grand in its wild magnificence—like some Alpine crag, with the pines on its slopes and the deep dark lake at its foot; he had courage, resolution, an iron will, a loftiness of soul that could hold commerce with the unseen and eternal. He was a man of vast heights and depths. He could hold fellowship with the eternal God as a man speaks with his friend, and could suffer unutterable agonies in self-questioning and depression. But is this the loftiest ideal of character? Is it the most desirable and blessed? Assuredly not; and this may have been in the Saviour's mind when He made His notable reservations. To come neither eating nor drinking; to be stern, reserved, and lonely; to live apart from the homes of men; to be the severe and unflinching rebuker of other men's sins—this was not the loftiest pattern of human character.

There was something better, as is manifest in our Lord's own perfect manhood. The balance of quality; the power to converse with God, mated with the tenderness that enters the homes of men, wipes the tears of those that mourn, and gathers little children to its side; that has an ear for every complaint, and a balm of comfort for every heart-break; that pities and soothes, teaches and leads; that is able not only to commune with God alone in the desert, but brings Him into the lowliest deeds and commonplaces of human life—this is the type of character which is characteristic of the Kingdom of Heaven. It is described best in those inimitable beatitudes which canonize, not the stern and rugged, but the sweet and tender, the humble and meek; and stamp Heaven's tenderest smile on virtues which had hardly found a place in the strong and gritty character of the Baptist.

Yes, there is more to be had by the humble heart than John possessed or taught. The passive as well as the active; the glen equally with the bare mountain peak; the feminine with the masculine; the power to wait and be still, combined with the swift rush to capture the position; the cross of shame as well as the throne of power. And if thou art the least in the Kingdom of God, all this may be thine, by the Holy Spirit, who introduces the very nature of the Son of Man into the heart that loves Him truly. "He that is least in the Kingdom of heaven is greater than he" (Matt. 11:11).

11

A Burning and Shining Lamp

John 5:35

"John was a burning and shining lamp." In the original a great contrast is suggested between *lamp*, as it is given in the Revised Version, and *light*. The Old Version put it thus: "He was a burning and shining light"; but the Revised Version puts it thus: "He was a burning and shining lamp"; and there is a considerable difference between the two. In the first chapter of the Gospel, the apostle John tells us, speaking of the Baptist, that he was not that Light, but was sent to bear witness of that Light, that all men through him (John) might believe. "That was the True Light, which lighteth every man coming into the world" (John 1:9).

Jesus Christ is the Light of the World; and I believe that in every age He has been waiting to illumine the hearts and spirits of men, reminding us of the expression in the Book of Proverbs—and it is wonderfully significant—"The spirit of man is the candle of the Lord" (Prov. 20:27).

Men are born into the world like so many unlighted candles. They may stand in chaste candlesticks, all of gold or silver, of common tin or porcelain. But all are by nature unlit. On the other hand, Jesus Christ, the Light of men, waits with yearning desire, and, as each successive generation passes across the stage of human life, He is prepared to illumine the spirits which are intended to be the candles of the Lord.

So let Jesus Christ touch you. Believe in the Light, that you may become a child of the Light. Take off the extinguisher;

cast away your prejudice; put off those misconceptions; have done with those unworthy habits: putting them all aside, let Jesus kindle you. "Arise, shine; for thy light is come." "Awake, thou that sleepest, and arise from the dead; and Christ shall give thee light."

We are kindled that we might kindle others. I would like, if I might have my choice, to burn steadily down, with no guttering waste, and as I do so to communicate God's fire to as many unlit candles as possible; and to burn on steadily until the socket comes in view, then to light, in the last flicker, thirty, or a hundred candles at once; so that as one expires they may begin burning and spreading light which shall shine till Jesus comes. Get light from Christ, then share it; and remember that it is the glory of fire that one little candle may go on lighting hundreds of candles—one insignificant taper may light all the lamps of a cathedral church, and yet not be robbed of its own little glow of flame. Andrew was lit by Christ Himself, and passed on the flame to Simon Peter, and he to three thousand more on the Day of Pentecost. Every Christian soul illumined by the grace of God thus becomes, as John the Baptist was, a lamp. But there is always the same impassable chasm between these and the Lord. They are derived; He is original. They need to be sustained and fed; He is the fountain of Light: because, as the Father hath life in Himself, He hath given to Him also to have life in Himself, and His life is the light of men.

The Inevitable Expenditure. "He was a burning and shining lamp." *If you would shine, you must burn.* The ambition to shine is universal; but all are not prepared to pay the price by which alone they can acquire the right to give the true light of life. There are plenty of students who would win all the prizes, and wear all the honors, apart from days and nights of toil; but they find it a vain ambition.

This is pre-eminently the principle in the service of Christ. It was so with the Lord Himself. He shone, and His beams have illumined myriads of darkened souls, and shall yet bring dawn throughout the world; but, ah, how He burned!

The disciples remembered that it was written of Him: "The zeal of Thy house hath eaten Me up" (Ps. 69:9). He suffered, that He might serve. He would not save Himself, because He was bent on saving others. He ascended to the throne because He spared not Himself from the cruel tree. Pilate marvelled that His death came so soon, and sent for the centurion to be certified that in so few hours He had succumbed.

Paul gave freely of his best. He shone because he never hesitated to burn. Remember how he affirmed that he was pressed down, perplexed, pursued, and always bore about in his body the dying of the Lord Jesus, that the life of Jesus might be manifested in his mortal flesh. The price paid for the life that wrought in the hearts of his converts was that death should work in himself.

If you burn, you will shine. The burning and the shining do not always go together; often the burning goes on a long time without much illumination resulting from the expenditure. Those who are rich in gifts and natural endowments cast much, and the poor cast in all their living; this they continue to do, year after year, and none seems to heed the awful cost at which their testimony is given. In many cases, the saints of God have burnt down to the last film of vital energy and expired, and there has been no shining that the world has taken cognizance of. Their bitter complaint has been, "I have labored in vain; I have spent my strength for nought, and in vain." But even these shall shine where all faithful souls obtain their due.

Let us see to the burning; God will see to the shining. It is ours to keep in company with the risen Lord, listening to Him as He opens to us the Scriptures, until our hearts burn within us; then, as we hasten to tell what we have seen, tasted, and handled of the Word of Life, there will be a glow on our faces, whether we know it or not; and men shall say of us: "They have been with Jesus."

It was a wonderful thing how often God put His lighted candles in the cellar. We would have supposed that He would have placed a man like John on a pedestal or a throne, that his influence might reach as far as possible. Instead of that He allowed him to spend the precious months of his brief life in prison. And the lamp flickered somewhat in the pestilential damp. It may be that this is your place also. In the silence of a sick chamber, in the obscurity of some country parish, amid obloquy and hatred, you are doomed to spend your slowly moving years. It seems such a waste. Where is the light needed so much as on a dark landing or a sunken reef? Go on shining, and you will find some day that God will make that cellar a pedestal out of which your light shall stream over the world; for it was out of his prison cell that John illuminated the age in which his lot was cast, quite as much as from his rock pulpit beside the Jordan. "I would have you know, brethren," said the apostle, "that the things which happened unto me have fallen out rather unto the progress of the Gospel, so that my bonds became manifest in Christ throughout the Pretorian guard" (Phil. 1:12, 13).

12
Set at Liberty
Mark 6:27

The evangelist Mark tells us, in the twenty-first verse of this chapter, that Herod on his birthday made a supper to his lords, and the high captains, and the chief men of Galilee.

The days that preceded the celebration of Herod's birthday were probably filled with merrymaking and carouse. Groups of nobles, knights, and ladies, would gather on the terraces, looking out over the Dead Sea, and away to Jerusalem, and in the far distance to the gleaming waters of the Mediterranean. Picnics and excursions would be arranged into the neighboring country. Archery, jousts, and other sports would beguile the slowly moving hours. Jests, light laughter, and buffoonery would fill the air. And all the while, in the dungeons beneath the castle, lay that mighty preacher, the confessor, forerunner, herald, and soon to be the martyr.

But this contrast was more than ever accentuated on the evening of Herod's birthday, when the great banqueting-chamber was specially illuminated; the tables decked with flowers and gold and silver plate; laughter and mirth echoing through the vaulted roof from the splendid company that lay, after the Eastern mode, on sumptuous couches, strewing the floor from one end to the other of the spacious hall. Servants, in costly liveries, passed to and fro, bearing the rich dainties on massive salvers, one of which was to be presently besprinkled with the martyr's blood.

In such a scene, I would have you study the genesis of a

great crime, because you must remember that in respect to sin, there is very little to choose between the twentieth century and the first; between the sin of that civilization and of ours. This is why the Bible must always command the profound interest of mankind—because it does not concern itself with the outward circumstances and setting of the scenes and characters it describes, but with those great common facts of temptation, sin, and redemption, which have a meaning for us all.

In this, as in every sin, there were three forces at work:— First, the predisposition of the soul, which the Bible calls "lust," and the "desire of the mind." "Among whom," says the apostle, "we also all once lived in the lusts of our flesh, doing the desires of the flesh and of the mind, and were by nature children of wrath." Second, the suggestion of evil from without. Finally, the act of the will by which the suggestion was accepted and finally adopted.

Predisposition Towards Sin

Herod was the son of the great Herod, a voluptuous, murderous tyrant; and, from some source or other, he had inherited a very weak nature. It is a remarkable thing, how strong an influence a beautiful and unscrupulous woman may have over a weak man. And for this reason, among others, weakness becomes wickedness.

The influences that suggest and make for sin in this world are so persistent—at every street corner, in every daily newspaper, among every gathering of well-dressed people, or ill—that if my readers have no other failing than that they are weak, I am bound to warn them, in God's name, that unless they succeed in linking themselves to the strength of the Son of God, they will inevitably become wicked. Remember that the men, and especially the women, who are filling our jails as criminals, were, in most cases, only weak, but they therefore drifted before the strong, black current which flows through the world, and have become objects against whom all parents warn their children. With all my soul—and I have had no small experience of myself and of others—I implore that if you are conscious of your weakness, you shall do what the sea anemone and the limpet do, which cling to the rock when the storms darken the sky. "Be strong in the Lord, and in the power of His might."

It was the most perilous thing that Herod could do, to have that banquet. Lying back on his divan, lolling on his cushions, eating his rich food, quaffing the sparkling wine, exchanging repartee with his obsequious followers, it was as though the petals and calyx of his soul were all open to receive the first insidious spore of evil that might float past on the sultry air. That is why some of us dare not enter the theatre, or encourage others to enter. This is not the place to enter into a full discussion of the subject; but, even when a play may be deemed inoffensive and harmless, the sensuous attractions of the place, the glitter, the music, the slightly-dressed figures of the actors and actresses, the entire atmosphere and environment, which appeal so strongly to the lust of the eye, the lust of the flesh, and the pride of life, break down some of the fortifications, which would otherwise resist the first incidence and assault of evil. The air of the theater, the ballroom, the race track, seem so impregnated with the nocuous germs and microbes of evil, that it is perilous for the soul to expose itself to them, conscious as it is of predisposing bias and weakness. It is this consciousness, also, which prompts the daily prayer, "Lead us not into temptation."

Temptation. Satan's accomplice was the beautiful Herodias—beautiful as a snake, but as deadly. She knew the influence that John the Baptist wielded over her weak paramour, that he was accustomed to attach unmeasured importance to his words, and do "many things." She realized that his conscience was uneasy, and therefore the more liable to be affected by his words when he reasoned of righteousness, temperance, and judgment to come. She feared for the consequences if the Baptist and Herod's conscience should make common cause against her. What if her power over the capricious tyrant were to begin to wane, and the Baptist gain more and more influence, to her discredit and undoing? She was not safe so long as John the Baptist breathed. Herod feared him, and perhaps she feared him more and was bent on delivering her life of his presence.

She watched her opportunity, and it came on the occasion we have described. Towards the end of such a feast it was the custom for immodest women to be introduced, who, by their gestures, imitated scenes in certain well-known mythologies, and still further inflamed the passions of the banqueters. But instead of the usual troupe, which Herod probably kept for such an occasion, Salome herself came in and danced a wild nautch dance. What shall we think of a mother who could expose her daughter to such a scene, and suggest her taking a part in the half-drunken orgy? To what depths will not mad jealousy and passion urge us, apart from the restraining grace of God! The girl, alas, was as shameless as her mother.

She pleased Herod, who was excited with the meeting of the two strong passions, which have destroyed more victims than have fallen on all the battlefields of the world; and in his frenzy, he promised to give her whatever she might ask, though it were to cost half his kingdom. She rushed back to her mother with the story of her success. "What shall I ask?" she cried (Mark 6:24). The mother had, perhaps, anticipated such a moment as this, and had her answer ready. "Ask," she replied instantly, "for John the Baptist's head." Back from her mother she tripped into the banqueting hall, her black eyes flashing with cruel hate, lighted from her mother's fierceness. A dead silence fell on the buzz of conversation, and every ear strained for her reply. "And she came in straightway with haste unto the king, and asked, saying, I will that thou forthwith give me in a charger the head of John the Baptist."

Mark that word, "forthwith." Her mother and she were probably fearful that the king's mood would change.

It is thus that suggestions come to us; and, so far as I can understand, we may expect them to come so long as we are in this world. There seems to be a precise analogy between temptation and the microbe of disease. These are always in the air; but when we are in good health they are absolutely innocuous, our nature offers no hold or resting place for them.

This shows how greatly we need to be filled with the life of the Son of God. Is not this what the apostle John meant, when he said that his converts—his little children—could overcome, because greater was He that was in them than he that was in the world?

The consent of the will. "The king was exceeding sorry." The girl's request sobered him. His face turned pale, and he clutched convulsively at the cushion on which he reclined. On the one hand, his conscience revolted from the deed, and he was more than fearful of the consequences; on the other, he said to himself, "I am bound by my oath. I have sworn; and my words were spoken in the audience of so many of my chief men, I dare not go back, lest they lose faith in me." "And straightway the king sent forth a soldier of his guard and commanded to bring the Baptist's head" (Mark 6:26, 27).

Is it not marvelous that a man who did not refrain from doing deeds of incest and murder, should be so scrupulous about violating an oath that ought never to have been sworn? Looking back on it, can you not see that you ought never to have bound yourself, and do you not feel that if you had your time again you would not bind yourself? Then be sure that you are not bound by that "dead hand." You must act in the clearer, better light, which God has communicated. Even though you called on the sacred name of God, God cannot sanction that which you now count mistaken, and wrong. You had no right to pledge half the kingdom of your nature. It is not yours to give, it is God's. And if you have pledged it, through mistake, prejudice, or passion, dare to believe that you are absolved from your vow, through repentance and faith, and that the breach is better than the observance.

"And he went and beheaded John in prison." Was he

wondering why he was allowed to lie there month after month, silenced and suffering? Ah, he did not know how near he was to liberty!

Perhaps one last message was sent to his disciples; then he bowed his head before the stroke; the body fell helpless here, the head there, and the spirit was free, with the freedom of the sons of God, in a world where such as he stand among their peers. Forerunner of the Bridegroom here, he was the forerunner there also; and the Bridegroom's friend passed homeward to await the Bridegroom's coming, where he ever hears the voice he loves.

"And the soldier brought his head in a charger, and gave it to the damsel; and the damsel gave it to her mother." There would not be so much talking while the tragedy was being consummated. The king and courtiers must have been troubled under the spell of that horror, as Belshazzar when the hand wrote in characters of mystery over against the sacred candlestick. And when the soldier entered, carrying in the charger that ghastly burden, they beheld a sight which was to haunt some of them to their dying day. Often Herod would see it in his dreams, and amid the light of setting suns. It would haunt him, and fill his days and nights with anguish that all the witchery of Herodias could not dispel.

So the will, which had long paltered with the temptress, at last took the fatal step, and perpetrated the crime which could never be undone. The crashing of the tree to the earth has been prepared for by the ravages of the borer-worm, which has eaten out its heart.

If you have taken the fatal step, and marred your life by some sad and disastrous sin, dare to believe that there is forgiveness for you with God. Men may not forgive, but God will. As far as the east is from the west, so far will He remove our transgressions from us. Perhaps we can never again take up public Christian work; but we may walk humbly and prayerfully with God, sure that we are accepted of Him, and forgiven, though we can hardly forgive ourselves.

13

The Grave of John, and Another Grave

Matthew 14:12

We have beheld the ghastly deed with which Herod's feast ended—the golden charger, on which lay the freshly-dissevered head of the Baptist, borne by Salome to her mother, that the two might gloat on it together. Josephus says that the body was cast over the castle wall, and lay for a time unburied. Whether that were so, we cannot tell; but, in some way, John's disciples heard of the ghastly tragedy, which had closed their master's life, and they came to the precincts of the castle to gather up the body as it lay dishonored on the ground, or ventured into the very jaws of death to request that it might be given to them. In either case, it was a brave thing for them to do; an altogether heroic exploit, which may be classed in the same category with that of the men of Jabesh-Gilead, who travelled all night through the country infested by the Philistines to rescue the bodies of Saul and his sons from the temple of Bethshan. God knows where that grave lies; and some day it will yield up to honor and glory the body which was sown in weakness and corruption.

Having performed the last sad rites, the disciples "went and told Jesus." Every mourner should go along the path they trod, to the same gentle and tender Comforter; and if any who read these words have placed within the narrow confines of a grave the precious remains of those dearer than life, let them follow where John's disciples have preceded them, to the one Heart of all others in the universe which is able to sympathize and help; because it also has sorrowed unto tears at the grave of its beloved, even though it throbbed with the fulness of the mighty God. Go, and tell Jesus!

The Two Deaths

With John, it was the tragic close of a great and epoch-making career. When he died men said—Alas! a prophet's voice is silenced. What a pity that in a moment of passion the tyrant took his life! Let him sleep! Rest will be sweet to one who expended his young strength with such spendthrift extravagance! Such men are rare! Ages flower thus but once, and then years of barrenness! But as we turn to the death of Jesus, other feelings than those of pity or regret master us. We are neither surprised, nor altogether sorry. The corn of wheat has fallen into the ground to die, that it may not abide alone, but bear much fruit. Here, at the Cross is the head of waters, rising from unknown depths, which are to heal the nations; here the sacrifice is being offered which is to expiate the sin of man, and bring peace to myriads of penitents; here the last Adam at the tree undoes the deadly work wrought by the first at another tree. This is no mere martyr's last agony; but a sacrifice, premeditated, prearranged, the effects of which have already been prevalent in securing the remission of sins done aforetime. This is an event for which millenniums have been preparing, and to which millenniums shall look back. John's death affected no destiny but his own; the death of Jesus has affected the destiny of our race. As His forerunner explained, He was the Lamb of God who bore away the sin of the world. The Lord hath laid on Him the iniquity of us all.

But there is another contrast. In the case of John, the martyr had no control on his destiny; he could not order the course of events; there was no alternative but to submit. But, from the first, Jesus meant to die. For this cause He was born, and for this He came into the world. Others die because they have been born: Jesus was born that He might die.

What answer and explanation can be given to account for the marvelous spell that the Cross of Christ exerts over the hearts of men? Tears of anguish are changed into tears of penitence. The shuttles of a new hope begin to weave the garments of a new purity. No other death affects us thus or effects so immediate a transformation. And may not this be cited as the proof that the death of Jesus is unique; the supreme act of love; the gift of that Father-heart which knew the need of the world, and the only way of appeasing it?

The Two Graves
Men have alleged that the Lord did not really rise from the dead, and that the tale of His resurrection, if it were not a fabrication, was the elaboration of a myth. But neither of these alternatives will bear investigation. On the one hand, it is absurd to suppose that the temple of truth could be erected on the quagmire and morass of falsehood—impossible to believe that the one system in the world of mind which has attracted the true to its allegiance, and been the stimulus of truth seeking throughout the ages, can have originated in a tissue of deliberate falsehoods. On the other hand, it is a demonstrated impossibility that a myth could have found time to grow into the appearance of substantial fact during the short interval which elapsed between the death of Christ and the first historical traces of the Church.

In this connection, it is interesting to consider one sentence dropped by the sacred chronicler. He tells us, that when Herod heard of the works of Jesus, he said immediately, "It is John the Baptist—he is risen from the dead" (Matt. 14:2). There was a feverish dread that he would yet be confronted by the murdered man, whose face haunted his dreams. His courtiers, ready to take the monarch's cue, would be equally credulous. From one to another they surmised—"John the Baptist is risen from the dead."

Why, then did that myth not spread, until it became universally accredited? Ah, there was no chance of such a thing, for the simple reason that there was the grave of John the Baptist to disprove it. If Herod had seriously believed it, or the disciples of John attempted to spread it, nothing would have been easier than to exhume the body from its sepulchre, and produce the ghastly but indubitable refutation of the royal delusion.

When the statement began to spread and gain credence that Christ had risen from the dead; when Peter and John stood up and affirmed that He was living at the right hand of God; if it had been a mere surmise, the fond delusion of loyal and faithful hearts, an hallucination of two or three hysterical women—would it not have been easy for the enemies of Christianity to go forthwith to the grave in the garden of Joseph, and produce the body of the Crucified, with the marks of the nails in hands and feet? Why did they not do it? If it be said that it could not be produced, because it had been taken away, let this further question be answered: Who had taken it away? Not His friends; for they would have taken the cerements and wrappings with which Joseph and Nicodemus had enswathed it. Not His enemies; for they would have been only too glad to produce it. What glee in the grim faces of Caiaphas and Annas, if at the meeting of the Sanhedrin, called to deal with the new heresy, there could have been given some irrefragable proof that the body of Jesus was still sepulchred, if not in Joseph's tomb, yet somewhere else, to which their emissaries had conveyed it!

It is difficult to exaggerate the significance and force of this contrast. The disciples did not expect Jesus to rise. They stoutly held that the women were mistaken, when they brought to them the assurance that it was even so. But as the hours passed, the tidings of the empty grave were corroborated by the vision of the Risen Lord, and they were convinced that He who was crucified in weakness was living by the power of God. There could, henceforth, be no hesitation in their message to the world. "The God of our fathers hath glorified His Son Jesus, whom ye denied in the presence of

Pilate, when he was determined to let Him go. . . . But ye killed the Prince of Life, whom God raised from the dead" (Acts 3:13, 15). Thank God, we have not followed cunningly-devised fables. "Now is Christ risen from the dead, and become the firstfruits of them that slept. And as by man came death, by man came also the resurrection of the dead" (I Cor. 15:20, 21).

The Effect of their Deaths

What a picture for an artist of sacred subjects is presented by the performance of the last rites to the remains of the great Forerunner! There was probably neither a Joseph nor a Nicodemus among his disciples; certainly no Magdalene nor mother. Devout men bore him to his grave, and made great lamentation over him. He had taught them to pray, to know God, to prepare for the Kingdom of God. They had also fasted oft beneath his suggestion; but they were destined to experience what fasting meant, after a new fashion, now that their leader was taken away.

The little band broke up at the grave. Farewell! they said to him; farewell to their ministry and mission; farewell to one another. "I go back to my boats and fishing nets," said one; and "I to my farm," said another; and "We shall go and join Jesus of Nazareth," said the rest. "Good-bye!" "Good-bye!" And so the little band separated, never to meet in a common corporate existence again.

When Jesus lay in His grave, this process of disintegration began at once among His followers also. The women went to embalm Him; the men were apart. Peter and John broke off together—at least they ran together to the sepulchre; but where were the rest? Two walked to Emmaus apart; while Thomas was not with them when Jesus came on the evening of Easter Day. As soon as the breath leaves the body disintegration begins; and when Jesus was dead, as they supposed, the same process began to show itself. Soon Peter would have been back in Gennesaret; Nathanael beneath his fig tree; Luke in his dispensary; and Matthew at his tollbooth.

What arrested that process and made it impossible? Why did the day, which began with a certain amount of separation and decay, end with a closer consolidation than ever, so that they were, for the most part, gathered in the upper room; and forty days after they were all with one accord in one place? Why was it that they who had been like timid deer, before He died, became as lions against the storm of Pharisaic hate, and stronger as the weeks passed?

There is only one answer to these questions. The followers of Jesus were convinced by irrefragable proofs that their Master was living at the right hand of power; nay, that He was with them all the days—nearer them than ever before, as much their Head and Leader as at any previous moment. When the shepherd is smitten, the flock is scattered and this flock was not scattered, because the Shepherd had recovered from His mortal wound, and was alive for evermore.

If their eyes beheld and their hands touched the body of the risen Lord, we may be of good cheer. Their behavior proves that they were thoroughly convinced. They acted as only those can act whose feet are on a rock. They knew whom they had believed; and they had no doubt that He would perfect the work which He had begun. What He had begun in the flesh, He would perfect in the Spirit.

14
Yet Speaking

John 10:40-42

The people were inclined to disparage the life of John because there was no miracle in it. But surely his whole life was a miracle; from first to last it vibrated with Divine power. And did he work no miracle? If he did not open the eyes of the blind, did not multitudes, beneath his words, come to see themselves sinners and the world a passing show, and the Eternal as alone enduring and desirable? His life was one long pathway of miracle, from the time of his birth of aged parents, to the last moment of his protest against the crimes of Herod!

This is still the mistake of men. They allege that the age of miracles has passed. God, they think, is either Absentee, or the Creature of Laws, which He established and which now hold Him as the graveclothes held Lazarus. No miracles! But last summer He made the handfuls of grain, which the farmers cast on the fields suffice to feed all the population of the globe!

Let us not disparage the age in which we live. To look back on the Day of Pentecost with a sigh, as though there were more of the Holy Spirit on that day than today; and as though there were a larger Presence of God in the upper room than in the room in which you sit, is a distinct mistake and folly.

We have thought that He was not here, because He has not been in the fire, the earthquake, or the mighty wind which rends the mountains. We have become so accustomed to associate the startling and spectacular with the Divine that we fail to discover God, when the heaven is begemmed with stars, and the earth carpeted with flowers: as though the lightning were more to us than starlight, and the destructive than the peaceful and patient constructive forces, which are ever at work building up and repairing the fabric of the universe.

Do not look back on the Incarnation, or forward to the Second Advent, as though there were more of God in either one or the other than is within our reach. God is; God is here; God is indivisible: all of God is present at any given point of time or place. He may choose to manifest Himself in outward signs, which impress the imagination more at one time than another; the faith of the Church may be quicker to apprehend and receive in one century than the next: but all time is great—every age is equally His workmanship, and equally full of His wonderworking power. Alas for us, that our eyes are holden!

Let us not disparage the ordinary and commonplace. We are all taught to run after the startling and extraordinary—the painter who covers a large canvas with a view to scenic effects; the preacher who indulges in superficial and showy rhetoric; the musician whose execution is brilliant and astonishing. We like miracles! Whatever appeals to our love for the sensational and unexpected is likely enough to displace our appreciation of the simple and ordinary. When the sun is eclipsed, we all look heavenward; but the golden summer days may be filled with sunlight, which is dismissed with a commonplace remark about the weather. A whole city will turn out to see the illuminations, while the stars hardly attract a passing notice. Let there be a show of curiously-shaped orchids, and society is stirred; but who will travel far to see a woodland glade blue with hyacinths, or a meadow-lawn besprent with daisies. Thus our tastes are vitiated and blinded.

It is good to cultivate simple tastes. It is a symptom of a weak and unstable nature to be always in search for some

new thing, for some greater sensation, for some more startling sign. "Show us a sign from heaven," is the incessant cry
of the Pharisee and Scribe: and when the appetite has been
once created, it can never be appeased. Be content with a
holy ministry which does not dazzle by its fireworks, but
sheds a steady sunshine on the sacred page. Cultivate famil-
iarity with the grand, solid works of our English literature.
Avoid the use of extravagant adjectives. Take an interest in
the games of children; in the common round and daily task of
servants and employees; in the toils and tears of working
girls; in the struggling lot of the cleaning woman who scrubs
your floors, and the lad who cleans your shoes. Do not be
always gaping at the window for bands to come down the
street; but be on the pavement before your house with a
helping hand and kindly word for the ordinary folk that labor
and are heavy laden. It is remarkable that in all these there
are tragedies and comedies; the raw material for novels and
romances; the characters which fill the pages of a Shake-
speare or George Eliot. All life is so interesting; but we need
eyes to see, and hearts to understand. There has been no age
greater than this; there is no part of the world more full of
God than yours; there is no reason why you should not see
Madonnas in the ordinary women, and Last Suppers in the
ordinary meals, and Holy Families in the ordinary groups
around you—if only you have the anointed eyes of a Raffaelo
or a Leonardo da Vinci. If the world seems common to you,
the fault lies in your eyes that have made it so.

Let us not disparage ourselves. Remember that God made
you what you are, and placed you. Dare to be yourself—a
sweet, simple, humble, sincere follower of Jesus. Do not
seek to imitate this or the other great speaker or leader. Be
content to find out what God made you for, and be that at its
best. You will be a bad copy, but a unique original; for the
Almighty always breaks the pattern from which He has made
one vase. Above all, speak out the truth, as God has revealed
it to you, distorting exaggerating, omitting nothing; and
long after you have passed away, those who remember you

will gather at your grave and say, "he did no miracle—there was nothing sensational or phenomenal in his life-work; but he spake true things about Jesus Christ, which we have tested for ourselves, and are undeniable. Indeed, they lead us to believe in Him for ourselves."

Speak to others privately. When only two disciples were standing beside him, John preached the same sermon as he had delivered to the crowd the day before, and both of them went to the frail lodging where Jesus was making His abode. There is nothing that more deeply searches a man than the habit of speaking to individuals about the love of God. We cannot do it unless we are in living union with Himself. Nothing so tests the soul. It is easy to preach a sermon, when the inner life is out of fellowship with God, because you can preach your ideals, or avenge on others the sins of which you are inwardly conscious; but to speak to another about Christ involves that there should be an absolutely clear sky between the speaker and the Lord of whom he speaks. But as this practice is the most difficult, it is the most blessed in its reflex influence. To lead another to Jesus is to get nearer Him. To chafe the limbs of some frozen companions is to send the warm blood rushing through your own veins. To go after one lost sheep is to share the Shepherd's joy. Whether by letters addressed to relatives or companions, or by personal and direct appeal, let each one of us adopt the sacred practice which Mr. Moody followed and commended, of allowing no day to pass without seeking to use some opportunity given by God for definite, personal dealings with others.

The apostle Andrew seems to have specially consecrated his life to this. On each of the occasions he is referred to in the Gospels he is dealing with individuals. Did he not learn this blessed art from his master, the Baptist?

It is requisite that there should be the deliberate resolution to pursue this holy habit; definite prayer for guidance as one issues from the morning hour of prayer; abiding fellowship with the Son of God, that He may give the right word at the right moment; and a willingness to open the conversation by some manifestation of the humble, loving disposition begotten by the Holy Spirit, which is infinitely attractive and beautiful to the most casual passer-by.

The Voice of Experience

"I saw and bare record." John spoke of what he had seen, and tasted, and handled. Be content to say, "I was lost, but Jesus found me; blind, and He gave me sight; unclean, and He cleansed my heart." Nothing goes so far to convince another as to hear the accent of conviction on the lips of one whose eyes survey the landscape of truth to which he alludes, and whose ears are open to the eternal harmonies which he describes.

A Full Heart

The lover cannot but speak about his love; the painter can do no other than transfer to canvas the conceptions that entrance his soul; the musician is constrained to give utterance to the chords that pass in mighty procession through his brain. "We cannot but speak the things that we have seen and heard" (Acts 4:20).

Does it seem difficult to have always a full heart? Verily, it is difficult, and impossible, unless the secret has been acquired of abiding always in the love of God, of keeping the entire nature open to the Holy Spirit, and of nourishing the inward strength by daily meditation on the truth. We must close our senses to the sounds and sights around us, that our soul may open to the unseen and eternal. We must have deep and personal fellowship with the Father and the Son by the Holy Ghost. We must live at first hand on the great essentials of our faith. Then, as the vine sap arises from the root, its throb and pulse will be irresistible in our behavior and testimony. We shall speak true things about Jesus Christ. Our theme will be evermore the inexhaustible one of Christ—Christ, only Christ—not primarily the doctrine about Him, or the benefits accruing from fellowship with Him, but Himself.

Thus, some day, at your burying, as men turn homeward from the new-made grave, and speak those final words of the departed, which contain the most unerring verdict and summing-up of the life, they will say, "He will be greatly missed. He was no genius, not eloquent nor profound; but he used to speak about Christ in such a way that he led me to know Him for myself: I owe everything to him. He did no miracle; but whatever he said of Jesus was true."

The Power of Posthumous Influence. John had been dead for many months, but the stream he had set flowing continued to flow; the harvest he sowed sprang into mature and abundant fruitage; the wavelets of tremulous motion which he had started circled out and on.

Parents, put your hands on those young childish heads, and say pure, sweet words of Christ, which will return to memory and heart long after you have gone to your reward! Ministers and Sunday school teachers, remember your tremendous responsibility to use to the uttermost the opportunity of saying words which will never die! Friend, be true and faithful with your friend; he may turn away in apparent thoughtlessness or contempt, but no right word spoken for Christ can ever really die. It will live in the long after years, and bear fruit, as the seeds hidden in the old Egyptian mummy cases are bearing fruit today in English soil.

BOOK II: PETER

1
Introducing Peter
John 1

The contrast between the method of the Divine Worker and the human is specially apparent in the earliest stages. *Man,* with considerable confidence in his own powers of initiation and fulfilment, cries: "Go to, let *us* build a tower the top of which shall reach to heaven, so that we be not scattered abroad" (Gen. 11:4). *God* begins in secret, and works curiously in the lowest parts of the earth. He calls an individual from the crowd, trains him long and patiently, and finally makes him His partner, the center of a new unit, the channel through which He pours Himself forth upon the world. Man's method, more often than not, ends in a Babel of confusion; while God's, invariably, is consummated in the city of the Living God, the Jerusalem which descends from above.

The majority of those who, from time to time, have been called to this holy service, have been selected from among the foolish, weak, and despised ranks of the human family, that the excellency of the power might be of God, and not of man. There have been thousands of noble exceptions; but, as a rule, not many wise, or great, or noble according to this world's estimate, have been called. The hole of the pit that has yielded God His materials has been of common clay, and the rock whence His stones have been hewn of very ordinary grain.

It is not surprising, therefore, to learn that the leader of the apostolic band was drawn from the ranks of very ordinary people, and that the story of his life opens in the obscure village of Bethsaida, at the north west corner of the Lake of Galilee. The unadorned and simple homes of its fishermen were in striking contrast to the marble palaces of the neighboring proud city of Capernaum, which were erected by the large incursion of Roman residents, who were attracted to the locality by its equable climate and luxuriant natural beauty. The shore was lined with costly palaces and imposing public offices; the roads were filled with splendid equipages; and luxurious gondolas flashed to and fro upon the lake.

The Hope of Liberation

The native population probably held aloof from the manners and habits of the conquerors, though quite ready to take advantage of their wealthy patronage and custom. Under their breath they spoke together of the great days of Judas Maccabaeus and of Judas of Galilee, before whom even the mighty Roman legions had on more than one occasion been compelled to give way. To these echoes of the memorable past were added a strange anticipation and hope, which stirred in the breast of many, that the hour was near when the invader would be driven beyond the waters of the Great Sea, and the kingdom would be once more restored to Israel.

Then suddenly the land was startled and shaken with the rumor that God had visited His people. A company of pilgrims, crossing the Jordan by the fords of Jericho, had been arrested by a strange figure, gaunt and sinewy, the child of desert solitudes, who had accosted them with the cry: "Repent, for the Kingdom of Heaven is at hand." When released from the spell and able to proceed to Jerusalem, they could talk of nothing else. That strange figure, half Bedouin and half prophetic! That voice which rang with trumpet-note! That evident vision of the Unseen and Eternal, which illumined his face with unearthly glory! That he had no lodging but a cave! That his food consisted of locusts dipped in water and baked on the hot coals, with wild honey to make them palatable! Without wife or child! These things gripped the national imagination and thrilled the air, already charged with electricity.

The little children were told to reverence the name of John, the son of Zacharias, whose parents had passed through such strange experiences at his birth. Multitudes were baptized in the Jordan—confessing their sins; among whom we may surely include the brothers Andrew and Peter, and their life-long companions, James and John.

The Baptist's Influence

Peter was married, but marriage among the Orientals takes place early. He was, therefore, still in the prime of his man-hood. Strong, vehement, impulsive and self-assertive, he could by no means be accounted a saint. Would he so easily have taken to swearing, when the maid accosted him in the hall of Caiaphas, unless he had been addicted to the habit in early life? He was doubtless attentive to the duties and for-malities of his religion, attended the Temple feasts, paid his dues, and was morally respectable. He was satisfied that he was a not unworthy son of Abraham.

From his youth he was an ardent patriot. Like all his friends and companions, he was prepared to sacrifice every-thing he possessed to see David's race once more on David's throne. When, therefore, he and the others heard the tidings of the Baptist's appearance, they hailed them as heralding the new era. Might not this be the first phase of the kingdom which the God of Heaven was setting up, and which would never be destroyed, and whose sovereignty would not be left to another people, but it would break all other kingdoms in pieces, and stand for ever?

His friends shared these convictions and hopes. Taking with them a frail canvas tent to serve as a shelter, and a bag of coins for the supply of their simple needs, Peter, his brother, and their friends bade good-bye to home and craft and "went forth to see." They crossed the Jordan by the fords of Bethab-ara and joined the crowds who were streaming down the

Jordan Valley to the scene of the Baptist's ministry.

Beneath such preaching, Peter must have been deeply moved. It raked his soul. Beneath those words sin revived and he died. He felt then, as he confessed afterwards, that he was "a sinful man." Frequently, as in after years, he would go out alone and weep bitterly, and when on the Day of Pentecost he saw that vast crowd of Jews pricked to the heart and crying out "What must we do?" he knew exactly the agony of their remorse. Probably he was baptized by the Baptist, confessing his sins.

First Meeting With Christ
When Jesus was baptized he may have been present, but as yet his senses were not anointed to behold the open heaven or discern the descending dove. Or he may have been paying a brief visit to attend to necessary affairs of home and business. Certainly he was out of the way, when, on two successive days, the Baptist designated the Savior as the Lamb of God. But he was back again in the Jordan Valley on the morning following the day of his brother's memorable interview with the One whose shoe latchet the Baptist confessed himself unworthy to unloose.

Andrew and John had spent some hours in His holy company. They had been welcomed to His dwelling, had listened with rapt attention while He spake of heavenly things, had perhaps listened to His recital of the salient features of the Temptation from which He had just emerged, and had been told of His chosen method for winning back the kingdom by patient sufferings rather than armed force. As they listened their hearts had burned within them. They knew, with absolute conviction, that they had found the Messiah; and rejoiced with a joy exceeding all their experience.

Leaving Christ's presence, they said each to the other "We must tell Simon of all this, so soon as we can find him"; and, as was befitting, Andrew found him first and brought him to Jesus, saying, "We have found the Messiah" (v. 41). *Brought him*, as though it was necessary to overcome some hesitation.

The young colt is difficult to catch, as if it realizes all that the first lassoing may involve.

Peter was immensely impressed by that interview. This Teacher was so complete a contrast to his earlier master John. Perhaps the hardy fisherman may have been less attracted to Him than to the sinewy son of the desert. He may not have been immediately susceptible to the grace and truth, and gentleness and purity, the humility and selflessness of the Lamb of God. But if this was his first impression, it was instantly succeeded by one of awe and wonder, as those searching eyes looked into the depths of his nature, and Jesus said, "Thou shalt be called Cephas" (v. 42).

This is our Lord's method of making saints. When the heart is broken and contrite, as was the case with Peter, He speaks words of encouragement and cheer. He imputes righteousness where there is but the smallest germ of faith. He awakens our expectancy by indicating possibilities of which we never supposed ourselves to be capable.

"Ah," said Peter to himself, at the close of that interview, "He little realizes how fickle and wayward I am; now hot with impulse, then cold as the snows of Lebanon. And yet if He thought me capable of becoming rock, and evidently He does think so, why should I not, with His help, resolve to attain and apprehend that for which I have been apprehended?"

Thus our Savior deals with us still. He tells us what we can become by the proper development of our temperament and the exercise of Divine grace; and as He speaks He imparts all needed help. We become possessed with the Divine ideal, and laid hold of by Divine strength; and thus the weakest become as David and David as the Angel of the Lord, the reed becomes a pillar in the Temple, the stone becomes a rock and the chief of sinners the mightiest of saints.

2

Early Days
in the Master's College

John 1

The wonder of that first interview with the Lord must have almost dazed the mind of Simon, the son of John. The Baptist's ministry had already stirred his soul to the depths, but this fresh and gracious Personality, so full of grace and truth, had revealed possibilities for his manhood which had never occurred to him. It seemed incredible that he should ever become known as the Rock-man.

Already Peter's heart had opened to Christ's knock, never to close to Him again. His soul had turned to Him with passionate devotion. Let those who remember how it was with them when they first met Christ bear witness if there is aught of exaggeration in this statement. They who have once really seen His face can never rest content till they have apprehended that for which He has apprehended them.

Whatever may have been the fisherman's reverie, he was soon made aware that Jesus was minded to go forth into Galilee, and he resolved to accompany Him. The distance to Cana from Bethabara was some thirty miles, and the little group would start on their way in the beauty of early morning. Apparently they had hardly left the scene of the Baptist's ministry, when they encountered Philip, and the fact that it is expressly recorded that he was a native of Bethsaida, "the city of Andrew and Peter," suggests that the two brethren had something to do with the Master's discovery of him and his immediate response.

This first journey in such company was the beginning of many similar experiences, until that further day when He would lead them out as far as Bethany and be parted from their sight. But it left an ineffaceable impression; for as these newly found disciples walked with Him, and heard Him open the Scriptures, their hearts burned within them, and emotions were aroused too tumultuous for words.

When they came within sight of the little village of Cana, the white houses of which, embowered with verdure, beckoned to them as they climbed the slope from the rich Esdraelon plain, Philip seems to have hastened forward to announce his discovery to a devout friend of his—Nathanael.

Probably our Lord and His disciples remained as guests in his home, and Peter was introduced to a new friend destined to be knit with him in a lifelong companionship. But it was at the marriage feast to which they were all invited on the following day that he drank in the deepest lessons of the Master to Whom he had given his allegiance.

The Marriage Feast of Cana
Jesus led them to a village festival, where a group of simple peasants, principally drawn from the vineyards that terraced the adjoining hills, were celebrating a wedding. He sat there among young and old, the life of the party; His face beaming with joy, His words adding to the pleasure of the company, His presence welcomed by the children and greeted by the young lads and girls. This was an altogether new and unexpected type of holiness. Peter and the rest watched it closely, as they reclined with Jesus at the feast.

And Peter learned many things beside. That though the Lord addressed His mother with perfect respect, He was under direction from a higher source. That only a hint of need was necessary—*He* would know exactly how to meet it. That those who were called to cooperate with Him must always give Him brimful obedience. That what His servants drew as water would blush beneath His word into the wine of the Sacrament. That He would always lead from good to better, from better to better still. These were wonderful discoveries: and it was a happy group that left Cana when the feast was over. Jesus, and His mother, and His brethren, and His disciples went down to Capernaum. Apparently they settled that their home should be there; but as the Jews' Passover was at hand, they could not then remain many days.

Though probably the Master and His disciples traveled with their own families to the Feast, they met again in the precincts of the Holy City. Peter and the rest beheld with wonder their gentle and lowly Master cleanse the Temple courts as though girded with the power of an Elijah. They witnessed the signs that convinced men like Nicodemus that God was with Him. Probably, also, in that journey Peter and his friends had their last interview with their earliest teacher, who reminded them that he had never expected to be other than the Bridegroom's friend. "Do not grieve for me," he said in effect, as they visited him and remarked the diminished numbers that came for his baptism: "I am more than content. My joy is fulfilled. I am of the earth, earthly, and I speak of the earth; *He* has come from heaven and is above all."

Nine months were spent thus. Perhaps Peter paid occasional brief visits home; but he returned to assist the Master in the baptism of those who confessed and forsook their sins; "for Jesus Himself baptized not, but His disciples." Then, to avoid the increasing suspicion of the Pharisees, the Lord and His disciples returned through Sychar and Samaria to Cana, where apparently the party broke up. *He* returned to Nazareth, while *they* made for their several homes. This was probably necessitated by the gathering storm, that broke first on the head of the Baptist, whom Herod cast into the dark dungeons of the grim Castle of Machaerus across the Jordan.

For a further period of nine months our Lord seems to have been unattended. He probably was in constant touch with

His disciples and friends, but they were not openly associated with Him. He was quietly preparing them for the great future which awaited them, but was as yet veiled from their view. Finally, when the fate of the Baptist was sealed, and no advantage could be gained by further delay, the Master went forth alone, throughout all Galilee, "teaching in their synagogues, and preaching the Gospel of the Kingdom, and healing all manner of sickness and all manner of disease among the people; and His fame went throughout all Syria, and there followed Him great multitudes of people from Galilee, and from Decapolis, and from Jerusalem, and from Judea, and from beyond Jordan" (Matt. 4:24, 25).

Peter was aware of this mighty movement, and found it irksome to stay with his boats. He dreamt of Christ by night, and watched for His coming by day. Presently the morning broke, and the Master came along the shore. That day changed the entire current of his career, and the seed sown patiently through months of quiet intercourse began to yield fruit, first the blade. . . . So take *us* unto Thy college and teach *us*, gracious Lord, we humbly beseech Thee.

3

The Settlement
as to the Supreme Control

Luke 5

Nine busy months had passed. Single-handed, our Lord had been conducting His mission throughout Galilee with an ever-increasing popularity. His speed was quickened by the tidings that the Baptist had been "delivered up."

It was the early morning of an autumn day. The grey waters of the lake were beginning to laugh back to the sun, slowly rising from behind the eastern hills. The deep azure of the sky, the exquisite foliage of the oleanders, the autumn tints on the trees and shrubs that came down almost to the water's brink, the changing lights on the hills, the white glistening snows of the mighty Hermon, which, though far distant, seemed to dominate the landscape to the north, the sob of the brimming water, combined to make a worthy setting for the supreme event in the lives of the four fishermen who were destined to influence all history.

They had been friends from boyhood. They were partners in their fisher's craft. They were ardent disciples and friends of Him who was moving the whole country. His life, deeds, and words were always on their lips, as they floated together over the fishing grounds, while the stars kept vigil overhead. Probably they had been speaking of Him, as they drew to shore, after a night of fruitless toil. "Would they be seeing Him soon?"

They had disembarked, were rinsing out their seine-nets, and spreading them on the shore to dry, when they became aware of the approach of a vast crowd, which were thronging and pressing upon the person of their beloved Teacher and Friend. He made straight for Peter's boat and asked that it might be moored within one of the rock-lined inlets that indented the shore. There He sat and spoke to His congregation, many seated on the blocks of basalt, others standing, but all rapt and wondering at the gracious words that proceeded from His lips.

The inexorable command. When our Lord is about to fashion a vessel unto honor, meet for His use, whether it be of gold and silver, or of wood and earth, He has to establish His absolute authority and right to command. There can be no parleying or argument, no hesitancy or holding back. Spirit, soul, and body must be absolutely submitted to Him, at whatever cost. The disciple must leave all and follow Him. Just as He was prepared to suffer obediently even into death, so He requires of them whom He takes into the sacred circle of inward companionship that they should arm themselves with the same mind, so that they should no longer live the rest of their time to the will of the flesh, but to the will of God.

Probably Peter and the others knew this *generally*. They could hardly have been with Him so long without realizing the force of the significant words uttered by Mary to the servants at Cana: "Whatsoever He saith unto you, do it" (John 2:5). They were prepared to give Him their loyal allegiance in the realms of morals and duty but it was altogether startling and unexpected when, invading their own sphere, He assumed their own prerogative, and said to Peter: "Put out into the deep, and let down your nets for a draught" (Luke 5:4). For a moment we may dare to assume that Peter's obedience faltered; and he expressed his hesitation in the reply: "Master, we have toiled all the night, and taken nothing."

Peter had fished these waters from boyhood. There was

nothing in the craft with which he was not familiar. The habits of the fish; the hours and spots most suitable for taking them; the effect of climatic conditions: in all he was proficient. He would have hotly resented any interference on the part of the fishermen of his acquaintance; and now, he found himself suddenly confronted with a bidding which was contradicted by his experience, by the universal maxims and practice of generations, and by the bitter failure of the preceding night, which had left him jaded, weary, and out of heart.

He would be prepared to obey the slightest precept that came from the Master's lips; but how could one who had spent his days in the carpenter's workshop of a mountain village be competent to take command of a boat and direct the casting of a net! Was he to renounce himself in this also? The morning was no time for fishing; the glare of light revealed the meshes of the nets, and the fish were to be found, not in the deep, but the shallower part of the lake. The whole of the fisherfolk that might see his boat putting out at such an hour, laden with nets, and evidently prepared for fishing, would laugh and count him crazy. Is it not thus with all who have been greatly used by Christ? There is no escaping the test. At a certain moment in our experience, often long after we have become disciples, the Master comes on board the ship of our life and assumes supreme control. For a moment or an hour there may be question and hesitation. We have been wont to make our own plans, follow our own chart, take our own course, and be masters in our own craft; shall we—may we, dare we—hand over the entire command to Christ? To what point may He not steer us! On what venture may He not engage us! At what inhospitable part of the shore may He not land us! Happy are we if, after such a moment of hesitation we reply: "Nevertheless, at Thy command I will put out even to the deep, and let down the nets for a draught." This at least is certain beyond doubt, that you can never reckon on Christ's co-partnership and blessing unless you are prepared to sail under His orders, and, like the angels, fulfill His commandments, hearkening unto the voice of His word.

Directly the Lord takes control, He steers towards the Deep of the Eternal Council Chamber, where we were chosen in Christ before the world began. The Deep of the Eternal Love, which loved us when we were yet sinners. The Deep of Fellowship and Unity with God, like that between the Father and the Son. The Deep workings of Providence which underlie all human history. The Deep Bliss of Eternity into which Love, which loved us when we were yet sinners. The Deep of Fellowship and Unity with God, like that between the Father and the Son. The Deep workings of Providence which unerlie all human history. The Deep Bliss of Eternity into which our restless souls will enter. The Spirit searcheth all things, even the deep things of God, and He will reveal them unto those that love Him.

But here we are specially concerned with *the Deep of Divine Partnership*. To Peter's surprise the boat, propelled by oar or sail, had passed over many well-known fishing grounds, and had kept its course to the midst of the lake, before our Lord bade them let down the nets. Immediately all hands were set to work, and the necessary preparations were hardly completed, when it was evident that they had netted a great shoal of fish. So much so that the nets were strained to breaking-point. The beads of perspiration were thick on his forehead, and his muscles stood out as whipcord, as Peter strove to cope with his spoils. His boat was lurching dangerously, and he made urgent signals for his partners, who apparently had put out in expectation that something of this kind would take place. And they came and filled both the boats, so that the gunwales were almost level with the water. Then Peter realized for the first time what partnership with Christ means, and how absolute obedience on our part secures absolute cooperation on His.

On the Day of Pentecost Peter again let down his net, this time into the vast excited crowds, and again the Lord repeated the miracle of the Galilean lake, and filled his net with three thousand souls. In the house of Cornelius his net had hardly touched the water, when the shoal filled the net. "As I began to speak . . . the Holy Spirit fell" (Acts 11:15). Surely on each occasion the Apostle must have looked into the face of Jesus with a happy smile, and said: "Ah! Lord, here is the Lake of Galilee over again."

This experience might be ours, on similar conditions. If it is not so, let us inquire for the reason. It lies, not with the Master, but with ourselves, our obedience, or our nets. If our nets are our addresses, sermons, or methods, we must make and mend them by careful study and earnest prayer. The meshes must be so closely articulated that no fish shall get through them. No pains should be spared so to present the Gospel as that our hearers may be without excuse. No vague and flimsy presentation of eternal truth is permissible. Mend your old nets, or make new ones.

Be sure also that they are clean. Wash out the sandgrit or weed that may have accumulated. Especially eliminate self. There must be nothing to attract your hearers from your message to yourself; and when you have done all, dare to believe that, though your Lord is now seated at the right hand of God, He is still working with His servants and confirming their word by the power of the Holy Ghost.

4

A Fisher of Men

Matthew 4

The Master's purpose for His disciples is disclosed in the words recorded by Matthew and Mark, and which were probably addressed to them on the shore, when they had again beached their boats: "Come ye after Me, and I will make you to become fishers of men" (Matt. 4:19; Mk. 1:17).

The summons came while they were engaged in their usual occupation. David was summoned from the sheepfold to shepherd the chosen race. Paul was called from making the goat's-hair tents to teach the Church the ephemeral character of the things that are seen, in view of the House not made with hands, eternal in the heavens. It was quite befitting, therefore, that our Lord should explain to His fisher friend the momentous and glorious ministry that awaited him, through the calling in which he had been engaged from boyhood, and which had so many points of resemblance with the work of winning souls. The one difference being brought out in the Greek word translated *catch*, and which should be expanded to read, as in 2 Tim. 2:26, "Thou shalt catch, *in order to keep alive*."

Knowledge of Personal Sinfulness

Many instances present themselves from the biographies of the saints. But two will suffice. The untiring and extraordinary labors of the great Apostle of the Gentiles laid the foundations of the Gentile Church, but as he reviews the past and considers his natural condition, he does not hesitate to speak of himself as the chief of sinners and the least of saints. John Bunyan's review of his condition, as it stood revealed in the light of God, is typical of many others, who shine as stars in the firmament of successful soul winning. He says: "I was more loathsome in mine own eyes than was a toad; and I thought I was so in God's eyes also. I could have changed my heart with anyone."

The ringleaders in the devil's army make great soldiers for Christ. Their knowledge of Satan's stratagems and wiles is invaluable. Reclaimed poachers are notoriously the best gamekeepers. The sinner knows the bitterness of the wages of sin, as an unfallen angel or an innocent child cannot. We need not be surprised, therefore, at this preparatory revelation of Himself given to Peter.

He and the rest had known the Lord for at least eighteen months, but were unaware of His true majesty and glory. For them He was the carpenter of Nazareth, the holy man, the marvelous teacher and wonderworker.

Then most suddenly and unexpectedly this shaft of His essential being struck into their ordinary commonplace, and left a trail of supernatural glory. For a moment Peter was dazzled, almost blinded. He could hardly see for the splendor of that light; but as he felt the tug and pull of the bursting net, threatening to break beneath its burden, he realized in a moment that his Teacher and Friend must have put forth a power which no mortal could wield. God was in the place, and he had not known it. How dreadful was that place! It was none other than the house of God and the gate of heaven; and at once the nakedness and sinfulness of his own heart were laid bare, and he cried: "I am a sinful man, O Lord" (Luke 5:8). Note the significant exchange! When the boat left the shore it was *Master*, now, as this revelation has broken on him, it is *Lord*. Immediately on this Jesus said: "From henceforth thou shalt catch men."

Whenever, therefore, this experience befalls, it may be deemed as preparatory to new success in soul winning. Ex-

pect to hear the Lord answer your confession of lowly sinnership with a new summons to take your boat and net for a
draught. The whole progress of the divine life within the
soul is characterized by confessions. We are always being led
to detect the presence of sin and evil in depths and motions,
which once seemed comparatively harmless and innocent.
Do not be afraid to know yourself beneath the Spirit's teaching; it is all preparatory to a new departure in "man-
catching."

Failure and Sin

"Depart from me," cried the conscience-stricken disciple. It
was as though he said: "I will bring Thee, Lord, to the spot
where I took Thee on board this morning; and when I have
landed Thee, Thou must go Thy way and I mine. I shall ever
love Thee and think of Thee as I float under these skies by
day and night, but I am not fit to keep Thee company." And
under his breath he may have whispered to himself: "But I
know not how I shall live without Thee. To whom can I turn?
Thou only hast the words of eternal life."

"Nay," said our Lord in effect, "that need not be. When
sin is repented of: abhorred, and confessed, it need not
debar from My presence or service. I can do with sinful men,
who are conscious of their sinnership. No sin is too inveterate but that I can cope with it, too foul but that I can cleanse.
Stay with Me, I will cleanse, heal, and save thee, and make
thee the instrument of saving thousands of sinners like
thyself."

A Consuming Passion

It cannot be one interest among many. The Apostle said
truly, "One thing I do." "They left all and followed Him."
We can imagine that after this moving exchange of words
Peter returned to his place to think over the marvel of the life
that now opened before him.

We cannot suppose that Peter at once entered into the Master's passion for the souls of men. That was acquired after-

wards. In the first instance he was content to follow *Him*, to listen to His words, to become His companion and helper. But it could not have been long before he and his companions began to be imbued with the same passion, until it became the master motive of their existence.

So it will be with ourselves. As we walk with Christ, by the constant aid of the Holy Spirit, we shall be conformed to His image. His thoughts and yearnings will be transmitted to us by a Divine sympathy. We shall long to see Him honored, loved, and exalted. We shall desire that He shall see of the travail of His soul and be satisfied. We shall become identified with His interests, and with no backward look on ourselves. The Holy Spirit will blow these sparks into a flame, and our life will be spent as that of Peter, who by his love for Christ was qualified to feed His sheep and lambs.

Let us ask that we may become partners with Christ in His great passion for men.

5

Primer Lessons

Matthew 4

The Ephesian church was reminded by the Apostle of having been taught by the Lord Himself, "as the truth is in Jesus." It is therefore of extreme interest to study the earliest lessons with which our Lord commenced to prepare Peter and his friends for their lifework. Everyone who desires to be a soul winner should sit in this lowest form in the Master's school.

The First Lesson

It befell thus. On what was not improbably the first Sabbath after their final resolve to identify themselves with Jesus, the little group of fishermen, whose action was widely discussed all round the lake, giving them a considerable amount of notoriety, accompanied Him to the usual synagogue service. When the customary exercises were concluded, their Leader and Friend was invited to address the congregation, and as He proceeded in words of spirit and life to unfold the mysteries of the Kingdom, the sharp contrast between His address and the dull deliverances of the Scribes to which they were accustomed struck them with astonishment. The contrast was as marked as between the sparkle of a waterfall and the stagnant water of a pit. "He taught them as one that had authority" (Matt. 7:29). Their hearts and consciences answered back with an echoing response.

The hush of the enthralled assembly was suddenly broken

by the cry of a man's voice. It seemed as though a captive and unwilling soul was made the organ of an alien and compelling spirit. "Let us alone," was the demand. "What have we to do with Thee, Jesus of Nazareth? I know Thee who Thou art" (Mark 1:24). This unclean spirit, or demon, may have tenanted that man's body and mind for years, unsuspected by his most intimate associates. But the near presence of the Divine Holiness, though curtained by the unrent veil of His flesh, extorted an involuntary but irresistible outcry.

The disturbance caused by that wailing cry from the abyss must have been very startling. The man may, up to that moment, have been regarded as a respectable member of society. No one suspected the duality of his nature; but Peter must have suddenly realized that the type of character, for which his Master stood, dominated as it was by the Spirit of God, and essentially holy, must discover, arouse, and call into hostility the whole kingdom of evil spirits, which Christ afterwards described as the gates of hell, or Hades. The warfare for which he had enlisted was not against flesh and blood, but against the wicked spirits that rule the darkness of this world.

The Second Lesson

Peter was strong, forceful, vehement. His voice would be loud, his tread heavy. His touch was not gentle enough for straightening bruised reeds. A considerable amount of training would have to be expended on him before he could commend, as he does in his epistles, compassion, pitifulness, and courtesy. It was necessary for him to *taste* that the Lord was gracious and to become clothed with that meek and quiet spirit, which is of great price (1 Pet. 2:3; 3:4, 8). The first lesson in this art was given in his own home.

After the amazing scene witnessed in the synagogue the Lord accepted the invitation of Peter and Andrew to come to the home, which they occupied in common, for rest and refreshment. James and John were included in the invitation. Probably some suggestions of this had been made previously, and the women of the household had been busily occupied in preparing. However, when the guests reached the door of the fishermen's home Peter's wife was on the outlook and taking him aside hurriedly whispered that her mother was down with "a great fever." She was lying on a couch in the inner chamber, with a dangerously high temperature.

"They told Him of her." Luke says that "they besought Him for her." But next to the marvel of her immediate recovery, so that she was able to take her part in ministering, they wondered at the tender gentleness with which the Master touched her hand, took her by the hand, and, as Peter subsequently dictated to Mark, raised her up. How little he realized that in after years he would do the same for a lame man on the Temple steps, for the beloved Dorcas at Joppa.

The world needs tenderness as well as strength. It is needed to touch the bleared eye of the blind, the seared flesh of the leper, and the feverish hand of a fever-stricken mother. Lives are blighted, homes are wrecked, and bright young hopes withered, for want of tenderness.

The Third Lesson
It had for long lain heavy on the Master's heart, and was constant incentive to the forthputting of the saving strength of His right hand. Nothing less could sustain His disciples, and especially Peter, in all future trials and disappointments. It was therefore arranged that the fronts should be taken off the households of this one city, that their compassion might be moved by the vision of the anguish of a single community, although in fair and prosperous surroundings. All that were diseased and possessed, together with their agonized friends, were gathered at sunset in the humble street where Peter lived. He could not have believed that so vast a mass of misery and pain was concealed so near his home; but it was easier to pass from the heartbreaking spectacle to plumb the fathomless anguish of the world. The veil, which never intercepts the view from God, but which is drawn before our eyes

lest life should be insupportable, was lifted for a few hours on the Sabbath evening.

When Jesus beheld the multitudes, we are told, He was moved with compassion, because they fainted and were scattered abroad. We must needs learn this lesson, if we would win souls. The first, second, and third prerequisite for life-work, such as angels did for Lot and his family at the gates of Sodom, is to be filled with the merciful compassion that filled their hearts. The broken heart breaks and heals hearts!

The greatest of soul winners in any age avowed that he travailed in birth for his converts, and was willing to be accused from Christ for his kinsmen according to the flesh. A speculum of ice may focus sunrays to a burning point, but cold hearts are not used of God to win lost souls. He preaches best who loves most.

If we are content to labor without conversions, we need not expect any. But if our soul breaketh with longing, or we can cry with Rebekah, "Give me children or I die," the answer will not tarry long.

The Fourth Lesson
In the early morning the household sought for their beloved and honored guest, but the chamber was empty. In vain they searched the house. Where was He? He had risen a great while before day and departed into a solitary place where He prayed.

Peter never forgot His Master's prayer habit, and he clearly determined to follow in those blessed footsteps. Pentecost came to him and the rest because they continued with one accord in prayer and supplication. The Sanhedrin was powerless to hurt because the whole company lifted up their voice to God with one accord. Prayer opened his way from his prison cell on the eve of execution. The vision of the Gentile world, cleansed and sanctified, was given as he prayed on the roof of the tanner's house.

John Wesley tells his preachers that their prime business is to win souls, and that only through unwearied labor and perseverance can they be free from the blood of all men, and he ends thus: "Why are we not more holy? Why do we not live for eternity and walk with God all the day long? Do we rise at four or five in the morning to be alone with God? Do we recommend and observe the five o'clock hour for prayer at the close of the day? Let us fulfil our ministry."

6

I Give Unto Thee the Keys

Matthew 16

For two years and a half our Lord had lived among His Apostles. Making Himself of no reputation, He had given them no certain clue to His dignity. To quote the words of His evangelist and friend, who more than any other penetrated beneath the Lord's grace and truth to their hidden fountain—"The life was manifested, and we have seen it" (I John 1:2).

Only six months of education remained before He was taken from them—a period during which His teaching must become much more intensive; and as a preliminary it was necessary to ascertain what conclusions they had arrived at, as the result of their observations and experiences.

In order to secure the necessary privacy for this all-important inquiry, our Lord journeyed to the extreme edge of the northern frontier of Palestine, where Mount Hermon, the chief Alp of the Lebanon range, lifts its mighty mass beyond the snow-line, screening off the northern blasts, and cooling the air, so that the dews of Hermon descended on the mountains of Zion.

The Master's Searching Question
"Whom do men say that I the Son of man am?" (v. 13). The answers were various. It was universally acknowledged that He was no ordinary man. People felt that a Divine fire was burning beneath the pure porcelain of His nature. But their

views were as various as the speakers. Some, with Herod at their head, expressed the belief—not without a shudder—that the Baptist had risen from his lonely grave beside the Castle of Machaerus. Others said that Elijah, whom Malachi had taught them to expect, had come to them in the "day of the Lord." Others traced a resemblance between Jesus and one of the old prophets. Probably our Lord was not specially disappointed or surprised by these replies. It was of small importance that conclusions had been arrived at in the Court of Public Opinion. He knew what was in man; and these inquiries were only intended to lead up to the second and all-important question: "But whom say ye that I am?" (v. 15).

Speaking after the manner of men, His heart must have stood still for the reply. And it came instantly, emphatically, and decisively from the lips of Peter, always the spokesman for the rest: "Thou art the Christ, the Son of the living God" (v. 16). The bluff fisherman had been taught the secret of the mystery which in other ages had not been made known unto the sons of men, as it was now to be revealed to the holy Apostles and Prophets by the Spirit. "Blessed art thou, Simon Bar-Jona (son of Jonas or John), for flesh and blood hath not revealed it unto thee, but My Father which is in heaven" (v. 17).

The Foundation of the Church

Then for the first time our Lord spoke of His Church. Notice the strong possessive pronoun *My*. As yet the Church—one, undivided, and hidden—existed only in the councils of Eternity. The future tense, "I *will* build," makes it clear that as Eve was builded out of Adam while he slept, so the Church was presently to be built from the death wound and the sepulchre entombment of Emmanuel. And it was destined to be His bride, His body, His fulfillment, through which He could manifest the complete glory of His nature. *My* Church! From eternity Christ loved her. By His blood He redeemed her.

The Church is the special object of hatred to the dark

underworld of fallen spirits, whom our Lord refers to as "the gates of Hades." Hades is the nether unseen world, the abode of the wicked spirits that rule the darkness of this world, under the leadership of "the Prince of the power of the air," who rules in the hearts of the disobedient.

Long and sore the conflict may be, but the issue is not doubtful. *They shall not prevail.* "The Lamb shall overcome, for He is Lord of lords, and King of kings, and they that are with Him are called, and chosen, and faithful."

The secret of the Church's prevalence over her foes consists in her foundation doctrine. Shall we not rather say, her foundation *fact?* Not the personality of an impulsive and fallible man, who within a few moments was to incur the sharpest rebuke ever administered by those gentle lips; but the Deity of our Lord, as "the Son of the ever-living God." The Greek phrasing of our Lord's reply leaves no doubt as to His meaning. Two Greek words are here. *Petros*, Simon's new name, signifying in Greek, as Cephas did in Syriac, a stone, or bit of rock, broken or hewn from its parent bed; and *Petra*, the Rock-bed itself. Our Lord carefully makes the distinction. If He had intended Peter to be the foundation of the Church, He would naturally have shaped His sentence thus: "Thou art Peter, and on *thee* I will build My Church." But carefully selecting His words, He said: "Thou art Peter, a stone, a fragment of rock, who under the power of God's Spirit has spoken with strength and certainty; but I cannot build on thee, for the foundation of My Church I must turn from Petros to Petra, from a fragment to the great truth, which for the moment has inspired thee. The truth of My eternal relationship to the Father is the only foundation, against which the waves of demon and human hatred will break in vain. No stone shall give. No bastion shall even rock."

The Gift of the Keys
It must be carefully noted that our Lord used the same words which He addressed to Peter also to individual believers in

Matt. 18:18, and again to His assembled Apostles *and others* who were gathered with them in the Upper Room on the evening of the Resurrection Day. See Luke 24:33, and John 20:22 and 23.

In the light afforded by these references we may extend the significance of this gift of the keys to include all who live and act in the power of the Holy Spirit. If we have received that blessed gift of the Comforter, as they did on whom the Master breathed that Easter evening, we also may wield the power of the keys.

This is the secret of the quest of the blessed life. Go through the world opening prison doors, lifting heavy burdens, giving light, and joy, and peace to the oppressed, proclaiming the Lord's Jubilee year. Shut doors opening out on the dark waters of despair. Unlock and open those that face towards the sunrise. For this is work that angels might envy. "Receive ye the Holy Ghost."

7
With Him on the Holy Mount
Matthew 17

On the afternoon of the last day of our Lord's sojourn at Caesarea Philippi He proposed to His three chief Apostles that they should accompany Him for a season of retirement to the upper slopes of Hermon. Little realizing what awaited them, they readily consented, and accompanied Him to a scene which left an ineffaceable impression. In his last days Peter referred to it as affording the outstanding evidence of his Master's Divine nature and mission. For him it was "the Holy Mount," where he and the others had been eye-witnesses of Christ's majesty, when He received from the Father honor and glory.

The Transfiguration
The place was clearly Mount Hermon. The vivid comparison, in Peter's special Gospel of Mark, between the Master's appearance and the snow, is an additional confirmation that Mount Hermon's snow-capped heights were in his thought. Here only in Palestine is there the permanent presence of snow.

The time was almost certainly the night. Our Lord was accustomed to spend nights on the mountains, which are the natural altars of the world. The overpowering sleep that mastered the Apostles, until the Transfiguration Glory was on the point of passing, also suggests the night season.

It is noticeable that the glory passed on Him as He prayed. In the case of Moses the glory of his face was due to its absorption of the Eternal Light on which he gazed. It was a giving back of what had been received.

The appearance of Moses and Elijah added greatly to the impressiveness of the spectacle. Moses was the embodiment of the Law, Elijah of the Prophets.

Only a few days before our Lord had unfolded, with graphic minuteness, the scenes of His approaching death. Immediately Peter, speaking for the rest, had sought to dissuade Him. "Spare Thyself," he said; "this shall not be for Thee." They were not able to understand or sympathize. Love, doubtless, and passionate devotion inspired this impulsive soul in taking on himself to rebuke his Lord. But, as on the Mount afterwards, so then, he knew not what he said. It was necessary, therefore, that redeemed humanity should furnish two of its strongest and noblest ambassadors to reinforce and strengthen our Lord, upon the human side, ere He set His face steadfastly to go up to Jerusalem to die.

The Topic of Conversation

"They spake of the *decease* which He was to accomplish at Jerusalem" (Luke 9:31). The Greek word is "exodus"—a term which struck Peter's imagination. In after years he employed it of his own death. "I must put off this tabernacle," he said, "even as our Lord Jesus Christ hath showed me; but I will endeavor after my exodus that you may have these things always in remembrance" (II Peter 1:14, 15).

It must have been a very startling rebuke to Peter and his companions. To them the death of the Cross seemed as unthinkable as it appeared unnecessary. Certainly He who had saved others could save Himself from such incredible shame and torture! Surely it must never take place! Neither God nor man could suffer it! Their Lord might have incurred the hatred of their religious leaders, but there need be no collision between Him and the Roman authorities, and these alone could impose death by crucifixion.

But now, to their surprise, they discovered that Heaven could speak of nothing else!

Clearly, the death of the Cross, which our Lord saw awaiting Him on the skyline, is the theme of Eternity. Every created thing which was in heaven and on the earth, and on the sea, and all things that were in them, were to be affected by it, and probably brought nearer the heart of God. Because He would become obedient to the death of the Cross, every knee would bow to Him, and every tongue confess that He was Lord, to the glory of God the Father. He would obtain the Name that was above every name; would put down all rule, authority, and power; and would win the subjection of all things to Himself, preparatory to handing all to the Father, that He might be All in all!

The enfolding cloud. Peter had made a suggestion, which was as ill-considered as it was hasty. In his account of this scene, communicated through Mark, he admits that he knew not what he was saying. It was a preposterous suggestion, which at least would make the Crucifixion impossible, that our Lord should disregard the claims of a lost world, and spend His remaining years in a tabernacle on the mountainside. According to Peter, Moses and Elijah were also to be detained from their blessed residence and ministry in the Upper Sanctuary. To think of these six living in rapturous fellowship on a high mountaintop, instead of coping with such scenes as that which awaited at the mountain-foot! Peter had much to learn, and far to travel ere he could write: "Who His own self bare our sins in His own body on the tree, that we, being dead to sins, might live unto righteousness; by whose stripes ye were healed" (I Peter 2:24).

While he was speaking thus he and his fellow Apostles beheld a cloud descending, which enveloped the radiant vision. From its heart the voice of the Eternal God was heard, bearing sublime witness to the Savior as the Beloved Son, and demanding homage from all. That voice was heard by the three awe-struck Apostles, and surely their solemn attestation to this remarkable testimony is full of reassurance and confirmation.

What might have been! As the sinless Man, the Second Adam need not have died. In a moment, in the twinkling of an eye, He might have passed with Moses and Elijah, through the open door of Paradise, to become the Patron, though not the Redeemer, of our race. Such a translation might have been possible; but if, at any moment, it was presented to His mind, He thrust it away, as He did when Peter suggested it, with, "Get thee behind Me, Satan, thou savourest the things of men" (Mark 8:33). For the joy that was set before Him—or instead of the joy set before Him—He turned His back on Paradise for Himself, that He might open Paradise for the dying thief and for us. And when the cloud had passed, He was left alone with His Apostles, and took the straight road to Calvary. In the words of Isaiah, He set His face like a flint, and we know that He has not been ashamed!

8

The Shepherd on the Watch

Mark 9

We must never forget that our Lord dealt with His Apostles, not only in a group, but as individuals; not in the abstract, but the concrete; that He studied their idiosyncrasies, and administered special correction or instruction as each required. His words, therefore, as recorded by the Evangelists, had probably a special reference to encourage or repress some trait of character which He had noticed. Each of that inner circle had strong personal characteristics, which must be studied and trained, before they were prepared for the special work which awaited them, as foundation stones in the New Jerusalem.

It would appear that Judas and Peter gave Him most concern. The one because his nature was so secretive and subtle, the other because his fervid and impulsive temperament was constantly hurrying him into extreme positions, from which he needed to be extricated. At one moment he would say, "Depart from me"; at the next he would leave all to follow. Now he has won the high encomium, "Blessed art thou"; and again he is addressed as Satan. In the same breath, "Thou shalt never wash my feet," and "not my feet only." Within a single hour he is ready to fight for the Master, whom he passionately loved, and denies that he had ever known Him. That such an one should ultimately be taught stability of character, enabling him to lead the Church in its conflict with a world-in-arms, presented a serious problem to his Master and Friend. He never doubted the sincerity of his affection, but was sorely tried by its fitful and impulsive exhibitions.

There were several particulars in regard to which he needed to be specially cautioned and strengthened.

The Struggle for Preeminence

Though Peter is not especially mentioned, we are not doing him a manifest injustice to suppose that he took a prominent part in the hot disputes which broke out from time to time, especially after our Lord's award of the keys, the reference to the significance of his name, and his inclusion with two others in that memorable Transfiguration scene. The probability of this supposition is confirmed by the fact, recorded by Mark, writing at Peter's own dictation, that when our Lord reached Capernaum, on His return from Mount Hermon, on entering "the house," which, of course, was Peter's, He asked them, "What was it that ye disputed among yourselves by the way?" (v. 33). At first they held their peace, for by the way they had disputed among themselves who should be the greatest. Then He sat down, and called them around Him, and said: "The only way in which a man can become first in My Kingdom is by being last of all and servant of all." Then He took a child—tradition says that it was one of Peter's own children, who afterwards became the Bishop and Martyr Ignatius—folded the happy boy in His arms, and said: "Whosoever shall receive one of such children in My Name receiveth Me" (v. 37).

Probably this ambition for the foremost place led Peter to insist that though all the others failed and forsook in the approaching hour of trial, certainly he might be counted on, "Although all shall be offended, yet will not I. Though I should die with Thee, yet will I not deny Thee" (Mark 14:39). And he meant every word he spoke. We have just used the word *ambition*; but there were softening, sweetening ingredients in his strenuous affirmations. There were present, at least, a passionate devotion, a resolve that no hurt, which he could ward off, should touch that revered body, and the inner consciousness that it would be easier and far better to die with Christ than live without Him.

In Respect to Forgiveness

On one occasion, when the Lord had been giving instruction on the duty of forgiveness, Peter broke in with inquiry, "Lord, how oft shall my brother sin against me, and I forgive him?" (Matt. 18:21) and further suggested that seven times was the limit, which he could not be expected to exceed. Then, in the parable of the unforgiving servant, which followed, sin against a fellow man was contrasted with the enormity of sin against God; and the Divine compassion, which releases and forgives debts of ten thousand talents, was described in glowing words, though the Divine Speaker said nothing of the cost in ransom blood which He would soon be paying in flowing streams from His own heart.

Our Lord knew, though Peter had no inkling of it, that an hour was near when His Apostle would find himself guilty of a ten-thousand-talent sin, compared with which the vilest affront ever received from a fellow mortal would appear to be but as an hundred pence; and at such time he would cling to the hope suggested by this parable, as a drowning man to the rope thrown out for his rescue.

May we not imagine Peter hurrying through the streets, on which the grey dawn was breaking sadly, and making for the garden, where only three or four hours before he had slept while his Master was in agony? How could he have said those terrible words? That he had failed where he had vowed to be strong, and had added oaths and cursings which had not soiled his lips for many years! That the Master had heard all! And that look! What could he say, or whither go? Should he take his life? Remorse was choking his breath. Then there stole over his heart the words: "I say not unto thee, Until seven times, but until seventy times seven" (Matt. 18:22). Did my Lord expect me to do so much, and will He not do the same? And did He not say that the lord of the servant was moved with compassion, released the poor debtor at his feet, and forgave a debt of ten thousand talents? Surely He must have meant *me!* And long after he wrote: "Love as brethren, be pitiful, be courteous, not rendering evil for evil, but contrariwise blessing. . . . He bare our sins in His own body on the tree. . . . Love covereth the multitude of sins" (I Peter 3:8, 9; 2:24; 4:8).

Reward

When the young man, unable to pay the price of discipleship, had turned sorrowfully away, Peter broke in on the Savior's disappointment with the question: "Lo! we have left all and followed Thee, what shall we have therefore?" (Matt. 19:27). Clearly the hope of reward was bulking largely on his vision.

It was as if our Lord had said, in answer to Peter's question: "It is true that thou camest early into the vineyard. Thou wert among the first. Also, thou hast borne the burden and heat of the day, and more also is to fall to thy lot; but when thou hast completed the task, thou wilt only have done thy duty, and thy reward will be according to the riches of God's grace."

This also in coming days may have afforded the broken-hearted Apostle some comfort, as he said to himself: "It is true that I was among the first to obey the Master's summons, but I have forfeited all right to reward, even if once I cherished some hope of merit: I am not worthy to be called an Apostle; I take my place with the woman who was a sinner, and with Zaccheus the publican; but the Master said that the reward was not determined by service, but by grace. It is not of him that willeth or worketh, but of God that shows mercy. God be merciful to me the sinner, and in me first may the Master show forth all longsuffering."

In regard to faith. In that storm burst which broke on Peter's soul on that fateful night, with what comfort must he have stayed himself on these precious words: "Hold on to God's faith; Reckon on God's Faithfulness; Dare to believe that He abideth Faithful and is not Unrighteous to forget." His own faith had failed, but God's Faithfulness was like the great mountains.

9

The Evening of the Denial

John 13

The Mount of Olives, during the Passover, was covered by a large number of families, gathered from all parts of the country, and from many lands. Unable to find accommodation in the overcrowded city, they provided for themselves slight booths or tents, their cattle tethered alongside, the maidens thronging to the well with their pitchers, while the children played under the shadow of the ancient olivetrees or visited the Holy City with their parents in an ecstasy of enjoyment.

It would be pleasant to think that our Lord was the guest of the dear home at Bethany, where Lazarus and his sisters loved to welcome Him; but it is more than likely that, after the Supper in the house of Simon on the evening of his arrival, He deliberately held aloof, lest His friends might become entangled in the web, which was being woven about Himself.

In the meanwhile the Passover was drawing nigh, and with it the treachery of Judas, the denial by Peter, and desertion on the part of them all. It is, however, with Peter's share in the happenings of the last evening of Christ's earthly life that we are now dealing. Jesus knew that the hour had come when He should depart out of this world to the Father. He knew also that He had come from God and went to God; and that the Father had given all things into His hand. With this knowledge was blended an overbrimming love. "Having loved His own which were in the world, He loved them to the end" (v. 1)—not only of time, but of the high-water mark of love.

It is practically certain, therefore, that He was more concerned for "His own," and especially for Peter, than for Himself. Hence the following precautions:

The Gift of Friendship

The priceless worth of friendship was a matter of daily experience with the Lord. He made no secret of the tender intimacy which knit His soul with that of the disciple whom He loved, and who, more than any other, has interpreted to the world the secret workings of His heart. He realized, therefore, how much a Friend of the right kind would mean for Peter in his abandonment to the black current of a remorse which threatened despair.

Jesus could trust John utterly. The ultimate proof of His confidence was given when, from the Cross, He committed His mother to the filial care of His beloved friend. Thus He knew what John would be to Peter in the hour of black darkness, and therefore threw them together in His last sacred commission. We are expressly told that He sent Peter and John, saying, "Go and prepare us the Passover, that we may eat" (Luke 22:8). Thus He set His seal on their old-time friendship.

Probably from the first they had been attracted to each other by an instinctive consciousness that each supplied what the other lacked. It is more than probable that each chose the other as companion when the twelve were sent out two by two.

It is not good that man should be alone, especially in hours when he remembers his sins, and is distracted with the inner warfare. The Lord anticipates such need, and before it arises provides a Jonathan for David, a John for Peter, a Timothy for Paul, a Melanchthon for Luther, a Burns for Hudson Taylor, and a Faithful or Hopeful for Christian.

A Complete Cleansing

With desire He had desired to eat that Supper with the chosen band before He suffered. It would be for His own comfort and strength, and for theirs. He therefore committed the necessary preparations to His two devoted friends, sure that no detail would be omitted which their love or forethought could anticipate.

The city was too preoccupied and crowded to notice the famous Teacher and His companions as they passed through the Kedrongate and made for the appointed meeting place. The walk had been hot and dusty, and all would have been thankful for the customary ablutions, common to every Jewish home. In this case, however, they were wanting. Ewer, basin, and towel were provided, but no servant could be spared from the household at that busy season. Would no Apostle perform this office for the rest, and specifically for the Lord? Apparently none volunteered. To arrest further discussion the Lord arose from the supper table, laid aside His outer garments, girded Himself with the towel, as any household servant might have done, poured water into the basin, and began to wash His disciples' feet, wiping them carefully with the towel.

A sudden silence must have befallen, as He passed from one to another in this lowly ministry, until He came to Peter, who had been watching the process with shame and indignation. "Dost Thou wash my feet?" he exclaimed; "my feet shall never be washed by Thee" (vv. 6, 7). How little he realized that a still more drastic cleansing must soon be administered by those gentle hands, or he could have no part with Jesus in the world mission of Redemption! "If I wash thee not, thou hast no part with Me!" (v. 7). Evidently Peter caught his Master's meaning. The outward was symbolic of the inward, the physical of the spiritual; and he replied: "Lord, not my feet only, but also my hands and my head" (v. 8).

It was as though he requested that his soul life might there and then receive a fresh beginning and that his entire being might be replunged into the fountain opened for sin and uncleanness. "Make sure work this time, my Lord, let me begin again, as I began at the first, with Thee in my boat!"

"No," said Jesus in effect, "that is not necessary. He who has recently bathed does not require entire immersion, if hands or feet are befouled. It is sufficient for the soiled member to be cleansed, and the body is every whit clean. When My disciples fall into sin, there is no necessity for them to commence their religious life afresh. It is enough if the particular sin, of which they are aware, is confessed and put away. Whenever that confession is made and that cleansing sought, I will show Myself faithful and just to forgive the sin and cleanse from all unrighteousness."

Peter must have been greatly confounded by this incident, when he lay under the shadow of his great sin. He was not a castaway. He had not forfeited his part in the Book of Life or in the Holy City. There was no need for him to begin from the beginning. The Lord would wash his soiled feet, and he would be clean every whit. God's work in his soul had received a setback, but it had not ceased. He need not enter a second time by the door of the New Birth; but he must turn again, and from his failure learn to strengthen his brethren. There was a world of difference between the apostasy of Judas and the backsliding of Peter!

10

. . . And Peter

Mark 16

An ancient tradition closely associates Peter with the author-
ship of the Second Gospel, which, while bearing the name of
Mark, was probably written beneath the prompting and
supervision of the Apostle. Graphic touches also abound
which were clearly reminiscences of one who had been an
eye witness of that wondrous life. In the forefront of these,
these two words may be cited. Matthew records the angel's
words to the women thus: "Go quickly and tell His disciples," but Mark makes the significant addition, *"and Peter."*
With the others, those words might be obliterated by tides of
time and change, but they were engraven on the rock of
Peter's character and inlet with gold.

In the Song of Solomon three traits are assigned to a perfect
love and each of these are notably present in our Lord's remarkable treatment of His Apostle and friend, who had been
warned thrice, had denied Him thrice, and on three different
occasions was restored.

Love is strong as death. Much had happened to our Lord
since that hour in the Judgment Hall when He turned and
looked upon Peter. He had drained to the dregs the cup
which the Father gave Him to drink, in pursuance of an
agreement to which they had entered before time cycles commenced to revolve.

His love is *strong.* In others it may be merely emotional and
affectional, expressing itself in smiles, or tears, or tendernes-

ses, and largely composed of sentiment; but Christ's love is strong as well as tender. He is Immortal Love, but He is the Strong Son of God.

Peter's Failure

"Watch with Me," He said, as He left them. The request was prompted by His humanity, for who does not know the priceless value of sympathy in the supreme hours of life? Could Peter ever forget the pathos of the Master's remonstrance which was addressed specially to himself—"What, could ye not watch with Me one hour?" But though Peter had failed Him, notwithstanding all his protestations, Jesus sent for him.

God's Plan Misunderstood

All the Apostles misread the situation. They had no doubt that Jesus was the Son of the Highest and the King of Israel. To the last they wrangled for the highest positions in the Kingdom. They were not altogether surprised at the approach of the armed band which, indeed, Jesus had taught them to expect. They had even provided against such an emergency by procuring two swords, of which Peter had one.

But notwithstanding all, and with the knowledge that his misconceptions were still clinging to him, Jesus mentioned Peter specially, and sent this special summons for him to come.

Peter's Denials

The band—their captive in the midst—turned back to the city. John first recovered from the panic-stricken flight, which had carried all the Apostles from their Master's side, and seems to have followed closely in the rear, while Peter followed afar off. John had gone "with Jesus" into the Council Chamber, the windows of which looked out on the quadrangle; but Peter joined the group around the fire. "He stood and warmed himself." He had lost heart and hope. That his

Master had so evidently refused his help had disconcerted him, and perhaps had created a veil of misunderstanding and disappointment. Still he wanted to see the end, and he thought to evade discovery by joining with the rest, as though one of themselves.

The portress, who had admitted him, leaving her post, came up to the fire, recognized Peter, and rallied him before the entire circle with the challenge: "This man also was with the Galilean." He was taken unawares, but parried the attack by professing that he did not understand what she meant— "I neither know nor understand what thou sayest."

Seizing a favorable opportunity, when probably their attention was drawn in another direction, he withdrew towards the porch, and as he reached it a cock crew in the grey dawn. While there he was recognized by another maid, who had probably heard the words of her fellow servant at the fire. She remarked to a group of bystanders: "This man also was with Jesus the Nazarene." Again he denied, and this time with an oath—"I know not the man." At the expiration of an hour he was back again at the fire, perhaps with the intention, made in his own strength, of retrieving the situation. He would vindicate his Master, even though he did not identify himself with His cause! But when he opened his mouth, his inability as a Galilean to pronounce the Hebrew gutturals gave the lie to his repeated and emphatic disavowals of any attachment to Jesus. One and another denounced him; his brogue betrayed him; and the kinsman of Malchus recognized his relative's assailant. The situation was extremely threatening, and the hapless disciple began to curse and to swear, saying, "I know not this man of whom ye speak" (Mark 14:71). But the more boisterous his speech, the stronger the evidence against himself.

A second time, while he was yet speaking, a cock crew, and Peter remembered the words that Jesus had spoken. Jesus also had heard, for the second time, the same sound, and had heard Peter's strident voice where He was standing. Then, forgetting His own griefs, He turned and looked at

Peter, not with anger or reproach, but remembering and reminding. And yet He sent for him. Many waters cannot drown His love! We too may fail Him, deny, and crucify Him afresh. But when our heart turns back in agony of grief and remorse, He will renew us again unto repentance.

Only they who have suffered keen remorse, as they recall some real or fancied lapse from the ideals of human love for those who have crossed the River, will appreciate the anguish with which Peter fled from the hateful scene of his denial. That last look of tender, pitying love haunted him! Could it be the last time that he should see that beloved face, or hear that familiar voice? Would he never be able to tell out his anguish and receive the assurance of forgiveness? Was this the end? Could he ever be happy again? Even if God forgave him, could he forgive himself? How could he have been entrapped in so false a deed? Why had he not kept away from the fire, or definitely left the scene when first he was recognized?

The Scene of Peter's Sorrow
Where did he go when he left the Palace of Annas? Surely to the Garden, that he might lie full length on the very spot of his Master's agony, and wet with his tears the sward which had been bedewed by the sweat of blood. And when the sun was up, and Jerusalem began to stir, he would make his way to the house of John, where he knew that he would be secreted even from the prying eyes of the others, who were bewildered with the events that had so suddenly swept their Master from their midst, and with Him all their hopes for the world and the next. At least they had this to be thankful for, that even if they had forsaken their Lord, yet they had not denied Him.

From his first Epistle we learn that Peter was an eyewitness of the sufferings of Christ. If, as is probable, that phrase includes the sufferings of the Cross, he may have stolen through the streets over which the midday gloom was beginning to gather, that he might, even from a distance and obscurely, see the outlines of the Cross, which bore the One whom he loved with all the passion of a strong and penitent heart. He might not tarry, however, for John probably awaited his return to care for Mary while he went back to stand so near the Cross as to hear the last dying cry which announced a finished Redemption and the committal of the Redeemer's Spirit to the Father.

With these details and others he returned home; and in the weary waiting time of the following hours Peter confided all the tragic story of his fall. Happy are they who under such circumstances have such a friend. Happy also are they who, remembering their own failures and weakness, are skillful enough to bind up broken hearts. "If a man be overtaken in any trespass, ye which are spiritual restore such an one in a spirit of meekness, looking unto thyself, lest thou also be tempted. Bear ye one another's burdens, and so fulfil the law of Christ" (Gal. 6:1, 2).

The Resurrection
Had the whole wonder and glory broken on the Apostles suddenly, it would have overwhelmed and dazed them. It was, therefore, wisely ordered that it should be tempted, and made "by divers portions and in divers manners."

The Empty Tomb
Early on Easter morning Mary of Magdala, breathless with haste, broke in on the sleepless anguish of John's home with her hastily formed impression that the body had been taken from its resting place by unknown hands.

Instantly Peter was on his feet and hurried forth, followed by John, and they made for the Garden at the top of their speed. On reaching the tomb first, because younger and fleeter of foot, John contented himself with looking in. Sacred awe, reverence, wonder, and respect for ceremonial custom withheld him. But Peter, regardless of all restraint, true to his impulsive nature, could brook no delay, but went straightway into the chamber whence his Master had gone forth an hour or two before.

The First Appearance

This was the next stage in the unveiling of the great wonder of the Lord's Resurrection; and evidently it made a profound impression on Peter, for it is in Mark's Gospel that we are told that when Jesus was risen early on the first day of the week He appeared first to Mary Magdalene, "from whom He had cast out seven demons" (v. 9). That last clause probably reveals the secret of the comfort which Christ's interview with Mary brought to his distraught soul. He well knew the story of her past, from which the Master had delivered her; and he reasoned that if Jesus had revealed Himself to *her*, had spoken *her* name in the old tone of voice, and had commissioned *her* to go to His brethren with the message of Resurrection and Ascension, there was good reason to believe that in his own case also, though all unworthy, the Lord would resume His old intimacy and comradeship.

The Message of the Women

They had departed quickly from the sepulchre, and ran to bring His disciples word; but they were arrested by the appearance of their Lord, who met them saying, "All hail!" They took hold of His feet and worshipped Him, and He repeated the Angel's bidding, saying, "Fear not, go tell My brethren." All this delayed them. It would appear also that, whereas Mary had gone to John and Peter, these women probably made for the other eight Apostles, who were gathered in the Upper Room; and as the Magdalene evidently hastened from the two Apostles to the eight, so the women hastened from the eight to the two, who were discussing the events of the morning, and even the Mother had staid her tears to listen with wondering expectancy.

The women broke in on them like a ray of the sun through a cloud drift in a murky sky. They had seen the Lord! He had spoken to them! He had commissioned them to bring them glad tidings of great joy! But before they met Him, the Angel had bidden them inform His brethren *and Peter* that He was risen, and was preceding them into Galilee, where they should see Him. The women had no idea of the relevancy of those words. They looked on Peter as foremost among the disciples, and it seemed quite fitting that he should be specialized by the Angel's message; but to Peter the mention of his name was as life from the dead. Did he not start up when he heard the women mention it? Did he not question them severely, to be quite sure that the utterance of his name was not an invention of their own? Did he not insist on their recalling and repeating the whole wonderful story, with every detail of light and shade? And when they had passed on to tell "the rest," did he not quietly adore the love that would not let him go, the love that bore all things, believed all things, hoped all things, endured all things, and that never failed, until it had found and brought back the sheep that had gone astray?

His Appearance to Peter
In his enumeration of the witness of our Lord's Resurrection in 1 Cor. 15 Paul records that "He was seen of Cephas"; and when Cleopas and his friend entered the Upper Room on Easter Eve they were saluted by a chorus of glad voices, saying: "The Lord is risen indeed, and hath appeared unto Simon" (Luke 24:34). That is all we know. Where they met, and when, and what passed between them—all these are hidden in Christ's heart and Peter's. Probably they will never be disclosed, even when the sea gives up its dead. Nor do we wish them to be disclosed, because we also have secrets with Christ, which we have committed to His safe keeping, with the absolute assurance that they shall never be divulged, even in that world where they know even as they are known.

What passed in that interview is not recorded, but from our own experience we can fill in the blank pages. We know that there must have been bitter tears, broken words, long breaks of silence when speech was over-borne, assurances that the penitent did really love, whatever might be argued to the contrary from word or act.

What delicate thoughtfulness there was in the Master's arrangement of this personal interview prior to the later gather-

ing of the day, when He revealed Himself to the entire company. In their presence Peter could never have poured out
his soul, or made full confession, or have kissed His feet.
That first hour of radiant fellowship cast its sheen on all
subsequent hours of that memorable day. Having washed in
the laver of forgiveness, he had boldness to enter into the
Holiest; and when the Lord showed His hands and side, the
credentials of His finished work, and breathed on them the
zephyr breath of Pentecost, Peter was able to appropriate
them to the full.

11

The Renewed Commission

John 21

Is there one of us who has not been entangled in some word and act which, if taken by itself, might have been interpreted as debarring us from future service in the Flock of Christ? But we knew in our deepest soul that such an interpretation would have been absolutely erroneous and unjust, since we were conscious that the failure was an exception, not the rule; an eddy or crosscurrent on the surface, not the main drift of the stream. Of course, there are sudden outbursts of evil which reveal an inward rottenness of long duration, as the fall of a forest tree may result from the prolonged activity of the borer worm at its heart. We must not forget to make that admission; but it is also true that under strong and sudden pressure a man may be betrayed into acts and words which belie his true self, as Peter's oaths, in the hall of Annas, belied his faithful attachment to the person of his Lord.

All things are naked and open to the eyes of Him with whom we have to do. Jesus knew that the Peter of the denial was not the real Peter, and since his future leadership depended on the concurrence of his brethren, He skillfully contrived to bring about a revelation of Peter's innermost soul, that the effect of his denial might be neutralized, and that unquestionable proof might be afforded of his possession of the qualities required for the leadership of the Church.

The evening breeze was fragrant with the myriad flowers of spring. Meadows and mountain-pastures were aglow with

color. The lake lay dimpling in the warm sunset. Boats and
nets were to hand; and with the eager alacrity with which
men will respond to the call of an old-time but long-
discarded habit, seven of them pushed off from shore in one
of the larger fishing boats, a smaller one being attached to the
stern, and made off for the familiar fishing grounds. Darkness stole down the mountains, the lights died out along the
shore, heaven's vault revealed its starry galaxies, the silence
of the night was broken only by the letting out and drawing
in of the nets, or the occasional stroke of the oar; but when
the grey morning began to break—they had taken nothing.

The disappointment was hard to bear. But those who have
had experience of God's dealings are well aware that one
door is shut that another may be opened, and that our program is arrested in a certain direction because God has provided something wiser and better. Had the fishers been successful that night, it would have been much more difficult to
win them back to a life of dependence on their Master's personal care. He wised them to understand that their livelihood was to be obtained, not be plying their fishing craft,
but by fires that He would light and meals that His own
hands would prepare. The lesson is for us all. If our days are
filled with consecrated service, we may go to our beds and
sleep in peace. "It is vain to rise up early, and so late take
rest, for so He giveth to His beloved in sleep" (Ps. 127:2).

They failed to recognize the Figure standing on the white,
sandy shore, enwrapped in the golden shimmer of the morning mist. Surely He was some early fish dealer; and the two
inquiries addressed to them across the quiet water failed to
dissipate their mistake. That fishermen, returning from a
night of toil, should be asked if they had fish to sell, or that
directions should be given for catching a shoal by one standing on the shore, were familiar incidents. But John, with the
unerring instinct of love, discerned the presence of the Lord,
and in a whisper passed his glad discovery to Peter. None of
the others could, for the moment, have understood why he
suddenly caught up and wrapped around his person the

outer coat, which he had cast aside to expedite his labors, and plunged into the water, regardless of the morning chill. Those swift strokes, however, gave him a brief additional opportunity of lonely personal intercourse with Jesus, in which to renew the ecstasy of the Garden interview.

We learn from the entire incident that, from our Lord's Resurrection and onwards, the seine net of the Gospel must be cast into the multitudinous waters of the human world, that the Master's presence and direction are absolutely essential to success, that the fisher's needs for comfort and subsistence would never be forgotten, and that when the Master and they have wrought together in obtaining the harvest of the sea, He will welcome them as they near the heavenly shore in the daybreak, and will feast with them and they with Him. None of them will then ask, Who art Thou? for they shall know that it is the Lord, and there shall be no misunderstanding or division, for the sea and morning mists will be no more, and the former things will have passed away.

The outstanding qualification for religious leadership are three: Passionate Devotion to Christ, Unfeigned Humility, and Indomitable Courage. In each of these Peter had been proved deficient by the incidents of the Betrayal night. But they were latent in his soul, as clover seed in an ill-nourished field, and only waited for favorable circumstances to call them forth. These circumstances and conditions were furnished by the Savior's loving thoughtfulness.

Passionate Devotion to Christ

Had it not been for the Denial, none of the Apostolic band would have questioned Peter's attitude toward the Master. The members of the other groups must often have longed for the ardor of the Boanergic group, and especially of Simon Peter. But a shadow of grave doubt now overspread the sky, and as they spoke together they may have questioned, with all seriousness, the strength and steadfastness of his devotion. Our Lord realized this, and knew that before He entrusted to him the tendance of His sheep and lambs, He must secure a very decisive and unquestionable expression of the Love which He at least recognized as a dominant factor in His Apostle's character.

Only those who love can satisfy the requirements of Christ's service. Therefore the Master asked persistently, "Dost thou love Me?" And to the thrice-repeated question Peter returned the same reply, "Thou knowest that I love Thee," only adding at the third time: "Thou knowest it not only with the perfect knowledge of God, but with the intuitive sympathy of man" (vv. 15-17).

Unfeigned Humility

Two Greek words stand for Love. The one expresses the reverent and adoring Love with which we should regard the Holy God. The other expresses love in its more human and affectional aspect. In His two first questions, Jesus asked His Apostle whether he loved with the former love. This Peter modestly disclaimed. "Nay," said he, "but I love Thee with the ardor of personal affection." Finally, our Lord descended to his level and asked if indeed he loved Him thus, eliciting the immediate response: "Assuredly, and whether as Son of God or Son of man, Thou knowest it right well."

With evident reference to Peter's boast made at the Supper, that though his fellow disciples might desert the Master, yet he never would, Jesus asked him if he loved Him more than the rest. But all his braggart boastfulness had gone, and he, by his silence and his grief, confessed that he dared not claim any priority in love. He was prepared to take the lowest seat, and own himself last and least. He had become as a little child; and our Lord did not hesitate, with the hearty assent of the brethren who stood around, to take him by the hand and place him in the old foremost position which he seemed to have forfeited for ever.

Indomitable Courage

From the beginning our Lord saw the Cross standing clear-cut on the horizon before Him. Amid all the excitement of His early appearance, He told Nicodemus that the Son of man must be lifted up.

This was our Lord's experience. "I have a baptism to be baptized with, and how am I straitened till it be accomplished?" (Luke 12:50). Henceforth it was to be Peter's also. "Thou shalt stretch forth thy hands, and another shall gird thee, and carry thee whither thou wouldst not. This, He said, signifying by what death he should glorify God" (vv. 18, 19). In his proud self-confidence Peter once said: "Lord, with Thee I am ready to go to prison and to death." The Savior replied: "Thou canst not follow Me *now,* but thou shalt follow Me afterwards." This *afterwards* had now dawned. The disciple was not to be above his Lord. He was to follow Him to prison in Acts 12, and to death at the end of all—the death of the Cross, as tradition assures us, and this prediction suggests.

The courage that could stand that strain was of rare and splendid quality, and approved his fitness for leadership.

By evincing his ownership of these three qualities Peter established his right to the foremost place in the glorious company of the Apostles, and he nobly fulfilled the position, as we shall see. He would have been glad if John's companionship and help had been granted him, and this yearning for his fellowship inspired the question, "What shall this man do?" But other work awaited the beloved Apostle, and would take him in another direction. "No," said our Lord, "John cannot be spared to you, but I will be your all-sufficient Helper to the end."

12

A Witness to the Resurrection

Acts 2

With his brethren Peter returned from the scene of the Ascension to the city with great joy. Though he must have realized that the blessed intercourse of the last six weeks was now ended, and that his Master had definitely gone to the Father, yet the indubitable evidence of His great power and glory, the memory of those hands outstretched in benediction as He went, the assurance that they were to be endued with the power of the Comforter within the next few days, and the assurance that Jesus when He came again, as He certainly must, would be the same unchangeable Lord and Friend as they had known Him, were sufficient to lift them all into an ecstasy of joy and triumph, which exceeded and overflowed their sense of deprivation. It was even as He had said, their Master had not left them comfortless.

Quite naturally they returned to *the* Upper Room, hallowed by so many precious associations. It may have been part of the house of the mother of John Mark, which afterwards became the gathering place for the harried Church; and probably it was filled to its utmost capacity when the entire group of Apostles, disciples, holy women, and the brethren of the Lord, was assembled. Peter seemed naturally and by universal consent to become their leader; but there is no sign of the autocratic power with which some would invest him. He simply acted as chairman or moderator for the time being, because the Lord Himself, though unseen, was recognized by them all as still literally present.

The one particular on which we lay stress is the definition which Peter gave of the special work which lay before them, as it had been outlined by the Lord during the previous days. They were to be witnesses to the fact of the Resurrection of their Lord. When their Master had said that they were to be His witnesses, Peter perceived that the one outstanding fact on which their witness bearing must be concentrated was His Resurrection, that carried with it all the rest and was the keystone to their position.

The Salient Feature of Peter's Lifework

It was witness bearing to the Resurrection. The word translated witness is fraught with solemn and sacred associations. It is *martyr*. So many of the early witnesses sealed their testimony with their blood, that the word became synonymous with the yielding up of life amid the horrors of fire and sword, of the prison cell and the ampitheatre. We cannot utter the word lightly.

The Resurrection of Jesus is not primarily to be argued for as a doctrine; it rests on attestation to a fact. It is, indeed, a gospel, a theology, and a philosophy. It was the fitting consummation of the work of Jesus. It satisfies the heart, answers our deepest longing, and harmonizes with silent analogies of nature.

Before our Lord entered on His ministry He was anointed with the Holy Spirit, and from the wilderness He returned in the power of the Spirit into Galilee. May we not say that He also tarried till He (so far as His human nature required it) was endued with power from on high?

If He was the Christ, i.e., the Anointed, how much more must His followers stoop beneath the chrism of Pentecost, that they might truly be known as Christians, i.e., anointed ones!

How often must they have quoted and pondered those parting words—"Ye shall receive power by the Holy Spirit coming upon you" (Acts 1:8). But they all continued together in prayer, with the women, and Mary, the blessed mother, and His brethren. Each day they expected, but for ten days patience was given the opportunity of perfecting her work.

It was the first day of the week, and a notable day withal, for the priests in the special Temple service would present the first loaves of the new harvest before God. That the fulness of the year had been safely gathered in was the subject of universal congratulation and thankfulness. The city was crowded with people from all the world. It was a time of house decoration, festal dresses, jubilant processions. It was the early morning, the embryo Church was probably assembled in one of the courts or precincts of the vast Temple area. They were all together in one place, when there was a sound from Heaven, as of the rushing of a mighty wind, which startled the entire city, and there appeared what seemed to be a globe of fire, which broke into tongues as of flame, that rested on each of them. The whole company were filled, and began to speak with other tongues, as the Spirit gave them utterance—Peter with the rest.

Meanwhile, summoned by the extraordinary sound, which evidently emanated from the Temple, a vast motley crowd gathered. It was composed of Jews and proselytes, religious men, gathered from every part of the known world.

Then Peter stood up and began to speak. His sermon was little else than the citation of long passages of Scripture, accompanied by brief comments, showing their application to the present hour; but the effect was extraordinary. As this Galilean fisherman began to speak, the mob suddenly became a congregation, the stormy waves of tumultuous emotion dropped into a calm, the minds of the audience were penetrated and subdued by the speaker's fervid eloquence, and the crowd became as one body, swayed and inspired by a common impulse. Presently the silence was broken by the cry as of a man who was mourning his firstborn, and it was met by the wailing as of a woman for an only child. The hearers were convulsed in tears, and sobs, and panic of soul, and from the entire congregation the entreaty arose: "Men and brethren, what shall we do?" (v. 37).

That anointing or infilling came to Peter at least twice afterwards, for the Scripture so teaches, but probably it came again and again. He was filled with the Holy Spirit on the Day of Pentecost, and a second time when he addressed the Court, and was filled again on returning with John from the presence of the Sanhedrin to their own company. Why, then, should we go on year after year without claiming our share in this Pentecostal Power?

There is not a single believer who reads this page who may not claim a share in the Pentecostal gift. Why not confess that it is your failure and fault not to have claimed it? Why not search out, confess, and be delivered from the sin or unbelief that has deprived you of your purchased possession? Why not humbly open your heart to the entrance of that blessed Spirit who changes the craven-hearted into courageous confessors, and makes the weakest mighty as the Angel of the Lord?

The Characteristics of Peter's Life-work

It was persistent. On the day of Pentecost in Acts 2; in his next great address, on the healing of the lame man in 3; in his apology before the rulers, elders, priests, and scribes in 4:10; by the great power with which he gave witness to the Resurrection of the Lord Jesus, in 4:33; in his second conflict with the Council in 5:32; in the answer which he gave to the inquiries of Cornelius and his friends in 10:39-41—Peter was constantly and consistently a witness to the same outstanding fact that though Jesus was crucified through weakness, yet He was living through the power of God.

It was steeped in Scripture quotation. We have already noticed this in the Pentecostal sermon, where out of twenty-two verses in the Authorized Version, twelve are taken up with quotations from the Prophets and Psalms. We meet with the same feature in the next chapter, where he refers twice to the predictions of the holy Prophets, that it behoved the Christ to suffer, and to rise from the dead the third day. It seemed as though a very special illumination had been given him by the Holy Spirit of Inspiration, that he might understand the Scriptures and perceive the relevance to Jesus of all things written in the Law of Moses, the Prophets, and the Psalms.

It grew in clearness of perception. Peter begins with "the Man of Nazareth approved of God." Then "Lord and Christ." Then "Jesus Christ of Nazareth." Then "His Son Jesus." Then the "Holy One and the Just." Then the extraordinary sublime phrase is piled as a climax and topstone on all the rest—"the Prince of Life."

Prince! He is royal, and deserves the homage of all the living. Prince of Life! There is a world, beyond the range of sense, where all live, and live unto Him! Prince of Life! In the literal rendering of this great word He is the Author and Giver of Life, so that he who believes in Him, though he has died, yet shall he live; while he that liveth and believeth in Him shall never die.

It was based on present experience. It is remarkable that in Peter's witness to the Master's Risen Life he does not refer to the spectacle of the empty grave, the ordered clothes, the Garden interview, the vision of His hands and side, the breakfast by the Lake, or the Ascension from Olivet. He says: You may judge for yourselves by *this,* "*which ye now see and hear.*" In other words, he felt that not only was Jesus on the other side of the thin veil, which hides the unseen world, but that He was doing things. He had reached the Father's right hand, and was sending the Spirit, as He promised. He was empowering them with boldness, insight, and utterance. He was working with them, and confirming their words with signs following. He was making lame men walk, prison-doors open, hard hearts to break. Peter said: "He whom ye delivered up and denied in the presence of Pilate, is alive, of this we all are witnesses, and *so is also the Holy Spirit.*"

Similarly a holy life will corroborate our witness to the

living Christ. If contrary to our former habit we seek the things which are above; if we manifestly derive from an unseen source the power that overcomes the world; if our joys abounds in pain and sorrow, like springs of fresh water amid the ocean; if though poor, we make many rich, being hated, we love, being refused, we entreat, being crucified, we invoke forgiveness on the agents of our shame—we prove that Jesus lives; like Stephen we must say: "Behold I see heaven opened and the Son of man standing"; and the angelic look on our faces must corroborate our words.

13

Peter's Deepening Experiences
of the Holy Spirit

Acts 2, 8

One of the greatest affirmations possible to man is that of the ancient creed, "I believe in the Holy Ghost." All knowledge, power, success, and victory over the world, the flesh, and the devil, depend on the recognition and use of the fellowship or partnership of the Holy Spirit.

He ascended that He might receive and bestow gifts on His Church. Of His fulness may all we receive, and grace upon grace. Indeed, unto every one of us grace has been given, according to the measure of the gift of Christ, although we must make the sad confession that we have failed to appropriate our respective shares in the Pentecostal gift. We have been satisfied with half-filled cups, when the river of God might be flowing through our lives.

Peter's Previous Experiences
On the evening of the Resurrection Day the Lord had breathed on him and the rest as they gathered in the Upper Room. "Then said Jesus to them again, Peace be unto you: as My Father hath sent Me, even so send I you. And when He had said this, He breathed on them, and said, 'Receive ye the Holy Spirit'" (John 20:21, 22). We gather, therefore, that their reception of the Spirit was directly intended to qualify

them for their mission. It was a distinct equipment for service.

Thus we learn that the filling, enduement, and anointing are equivalent terms, and are all associated with the service we are called upon to render. We may have been born of the Spirit, and have so received the seed of the new life, but we must also be anointed by the Spirit, if we expect to be fully used by the Master in our brief mortal life.

When our Apostle faced the Sanhedrin on the morning after the miracle of the cripple at the Beautiful Gate, we are told that on arising to reply to his accusers, he was again suddenly and gloriously filled with the Holy Spirit, proving that we may claim successive and repeated infillings, especially when overtaken by an hour of crisis.

Peter had also had repeated evidences of the convicting power of the Spirit of God. "When they heard this, they were pricked in their heart" (Acts 2:37). Of this quality in the blessed Paraclete we have many conspicuous modern examples. As he was dying, Brainerd said to his brother: "When ministers feel the special gracious influences of the Holy Spirit in their hearts, it wonderfully assists them to come at the consciences of men, and as it were to handle them; whereas without these, whatever reason or oratory we may employ, we do but make use of stumps instead of hands." So Peter had discovered.

Comforter of the Church

It became apparent in connection with the finances of the Church the multitude of them that believed were of one heart and soul, so that none of them claimed any of his possessions as his own. All was held as a common property. There was therefore no poverty or clamant need. Those who were possessors of lands or houses sold them, and brought the whole amount that had been realized and gave it to the Apostles, by whom distribution was made to every one according to his wants. Out of this fund a certain amount would be laid aside for the rooms and meals which they had in common.

If a handful of people, however obscure, gather in the Name of Christ to consider and further the interests of His Kingdom, the Holy Spirit is not only present, but He presides. He holds court as the Representative and Viceregent of Christ. He sees to it that in their unanimity after united prayer, the will of Christ is reflected, and that through their united action it is done.

The Co-Witness of the Holy Spirit

The public sentiment of Jerusalem was strongly in favor of the Church. This was largely accounted for by miraculous works of healing that gathered the crowds around the Apostles, as formerly to the Person of the Lord. In the early days of His popularity the people pressed to touch Him. "Wheresoever He entered, into villages, or into cities, or into the country, they laid the sick in the marketplaces, and besought that they might touch if it were but the border of His garment; and as many as touched Him were made whole" (Mark 6:56). Those scenes were repeated in the narrow streets of Jerusalem, that as Peter came by his shadow might be cast at least on some of the sick who were laid on beds and couches along his pathway. The tidings of the marvelous cures which were effected spread to the cities and towns round about and attracted immense multitudes to see and hear and be healed. The country rang with the tidings of the wondrous cures wrought in the Name of Jesus.

The Master had promised that this should be their experience. "When the Comforter is come, whom I will send unto you from the Father even the Spirit of Truth which proceedeth from the Father, He shall bear witness of Me; and ye also shall bear witness, because ye have been with Me from the beginning" (John 15:26, 27). There we have the Savior's own promise that the Church may count on the corroborating affirmations of the Spirit of Truth. When the voice is heard from Heaven, proclaiming the blessedness of those that have died in Christ, the Spirit utters His emphatic *Amen* in the hearts of men. In the story of Paul's first missionary campaign we are told that the Lord bare witness to the word of His grace; and in the opening chapters of the Epistle to the Hebrews we learn that God bare witness to the earliest Evangelists of the Cross by signs, and wonders, and gifts of the Holy Spirit.

As Peter put it in his address, it is when we announce Jesus as dying, rising, and exalted, as Savior and Prince, as the Foundation and Lord of life, that we may count most surely on the Divine Spirit endorsing and attesting the truth, as though He said: "It is so!"

The Spirit's Superiority

The Evangelist Philip had been the means of a marvelous spiritual revival at Samaria, and had there encountered in Simon a crafty and ambitious man, who was clearly adept in the occult learning of the age and in the black arts of sorcery and witchcraft. Miracles were wrought by his collusion with demon influences, which in our own time have revived under the name of Spiritualism.

Presently a demand arose for further help than Philip could give, and the Apostles, who had remained in Jerusalem, notwithstanding the persecution, which broke out after Stephen's death, that they might focus and guide the entire Christian movement, sent Peter and John to give on their behalf formal recognition to the infant Christian Church which had arisen from the gracious work of this Revival. During the solemn act which sought and obtained a further bestowal of the Holy Spirit, there seems to have been such a conspicuous manifestation of spiritual power as astounded the beholders and specially Simon. With amazement he beheld the exaltation that transfigured spirit, soul and body, and lifted the converts into unparalleled ecstasy. If only he could obtain the talisman of a similar power it would be worth a mine of gold; and so he hazarded the offer which has for ever stamped his name with the infamy, and made it, as Simony, the brand of similar proposals. Turning on the wretched and misguided man, Peter sternly rebuked him.

"Thy silver perish with thee, because thou hast thought that the Gift of God may be obtained by money. Thou has neither part nor lot in this matter; for thy heart is not right with God" (Acts 8:20, 21). But, as Peter uttered those terrible words, did there not break in on his soul, by force of contrast, a fresh and living conception, not only of the superlative power of the Holy Spirit, but of the divine purity and beauty of His workmanship, and of the absolute necessity that the character of those with whom He cooperates must also be pure and holy, free from the taint of greed, and able to receive His blessed help, with no selfish ambition, but as the humble and cleansed channels and instruments of His will? "Be ye clean that bear the vessels of the Lord!"

14
Life's Afterglow
I Peter 4

In his Epistles the Apostle stored the thoughts which he was especially anxious should be associated with his memory, and we must needs linger a little longer to consider them; and they may be thus enumerated:

Comfort Amid Trial
The Lord had especially commissioned him to strengthen his brethren, and indeed they were passing through experiences that specially called for comfort and strength. They were reproached for the Name of Christ. They were called upon to suffer as Christians. Their enemies spoke against them as evil-doers, and falsely maligned their manner of life. The trials to their faith, patience, and constancy were "fiery." They resembled the ordeal of scorching flame. In fact, they were called to be partakers of the sufferings of Christ, as though their path lay, as His had done, through Gethsemane and conducted to Calvary.

In these circumstances, what could be more exhilarating than the Apostle's repeated reminder of the example and constancy of the Savior, who had suffered for them, leaving them an example that they should follow in His steps? It was not a strange thing that had happened to them. Christ had once suffered as they were suffering, and they had every reason to be proud of their association with Him in His supreme and unapproachable death. "Rejoice," he said, "inasmuch as ye are partakers of Christ's sufferings."

The Savior's Death

That was no ordinary death before which the sun veiled his face and the rocks rent in sympathy. It was the death of the Redeemer. It was a sacrifice, as of a Lamb without blemish or spot. The Son of God had borne the sins of men in His own body on the tree. He had died, the just for the unjust, to bring them to God.

The element of sacrifice had always been present in the nature of God; and it was due to this that the Almighty was warranted in creating beings that could sin. But thence arose the demand that His children should be holy in all manner of life, while the crime of neglecting the love, which counted no cost too great, if only it might achieve salvation, was proportionately enhanced. If judgment began with the house of God, what would be the end of those who obeyed not the Gospel of such love, of such infinite value, of such unestimable price?

The Certainty of Future Glory

Those whom Peter addressed were reminded that they had been begotten unto a living hope by the resurrection of Jesus Christ from the dead. For them an inheritance had been purchased and was awaiting them, which was incorruptible, undefiled, and amaranthine. For them a salvation was ready to be revealed, which would cause them to forget their heaviness through manifold trials. Great Grace was to be brought unto them at the glorious unveiling of Jesus Christ. They had been partakers of Christ's sufferings, but His Glory would certainly be revealed, and then they would be glad with exceeding joy, and would receive a crown of glory that could not fade away.

If Paul may be termed the Apostle of Faith, and John the Apostle of Love, surely Peter is rightly styled *the Apostle of Hope.*

Holy Living

His converts were elect through sanctification of the Spirit unto obedience. They could not fashion their lives according to their former lusts, committed in comparative ignorance. He who had called them was holy, and they must be holy also. They were called to be a chosen generation, a royal priesthood, a holy nation, a people for Christ's own possession; and they must show forth the praises of Him who had called them out of darkness into His marvelous light. By their good works they were to compel the Gentiles to glorify God.

Thus the soul of the believer may actually become a partaker of the Divine nature, and escape the corruption that is in the world through lust. Thus also shall we be neither barren nor unfruitful in the knowledge of Jesus Christ our Lord. What a conception is here of the gallant ship having battled its way through storm and danger, coming into harbor with flags flying at the masthead and greeted by welcoming crowds!

The Nature of Death

He thought and spoke of it as the putting off of the tent or tabernacle, which symbolized the pilgrim-character of his earthly life, that he might enter the house not made with hands, his permanent dwelling place, eternal in the heavens. He said that it was a decease, or exodus. For him death was not a condition, but a passage. It was no Bridge of Sighs from a Palace to a Dungeon, but one of Smiles and Jubilation from a cell to the blaze of the Eternal Day. It was the crossing of the bar that lay between the limitations of the harbor and the broad ocean expanse.

He humbly hoped that he and those whom he addressed might have an abundant entrance ministered unto them into Christ's eternal Kingdom and glory. But beyond this he counted on the inheritance that was reserved in Heaven for him, and that he would be permitted to partake of the Glory to be revealed. But all was summed up in the vision of that dear face, which he hoped to see as soon as he had crossed over. Jesus had been the daystar of his heart, and Jesus would be the light of all his future, in the City which needs neither sun nor moon, because the Lamb is the light thereof.

BOOK III: PAUL

1
When I Was a Child

Acts 22, 23

Not far from the easternmost bay of the Mediterranean, in the midst of a rich and luxuriant plain, stood Tarsus, "no mean city," as one of its greatest sons tells us, but at the time of which we write a thriving emporium of trade, and a focus of intellectual and religious activity. On the edge of the plain, to the north, rose the mighty Taurus mountains, with their peaks of eternal snow, feeding with perpetual freshness and fulness the river Cydnus, which, after pouring over a cataract of considerable size, passed through the midst of the town, and so to the sea. During the last part of its course it was navigable by the largest vessels, which brought the treasures of East and West to the wharves that lined either bank. Here were piled merchandise and commodities of every kind, brought to exchange for the cloth of goat's hair for which the town was famous, and which was furnished by the flocks of goats that browsed on the lower slopes of the Taurus, tended by the hardy mountaineers. Tarsus also received the trade which poured through the Cilician Gates—a famous pass through the mountains, which led upwards from the coast to Central Asia Minor, to Phrygia and Lycaonia on one side, and to Cappadocia on the other.

In the Jewish quarter of this thriving city at the beginning of this era (perhaps about A.D. 4, while Jesus was still an infant in His mother's arms at Nazareth) a child was born, who by his life and words was destined to make it famous in all after

time, and to give a new impulse to men's religious convictions. At his circumcision he probably received a double
name, that of Saul for his family, and that of Paul for the
world of trade and municipal life.

The stamp of the great city left an ineffaceable impression
on the growing lad, and in this his early years were widely
different from his Master's. Jesus was nurtured in a highland
village, and avoiding towns, loved to teach on the hillside,
and cull His illustrations from the field of nature. Paul was
reared amid the busy streets and crowded bazaars of Tarsus,
thronged with merchants, students, and sailors from all parts
of the world. Unconsciously, as the lad grew he was being
prepared to understand human life under every aspect, and
to become habituated to the thoughts and habits of the store,
the camp, the arena, the temple. He became a man to whom
nothing which touched human life was foreign. He loved the
stir of city life, and drew his metaphors from its keen interests.

He came of pure Hebrew stock. "A Hebrew of *(sprung from)*
the Hebrews." On both sides his genealogy was pure. There
was no Gentile admixture in his blood, no bar sinister in his
descent. His father must have been a man of considerable
position, or he would not have possessed the coveted birth-
right of Roman citizenship. Though living away from Palestine, he was not a Hellenist Jew; but as distinctly Hebrew as
any that dwelt in the Holy City herself. Perhaps given to
sternness with his children; or it might not have occurred to
his son, in after years, to warn fathers against provoking
their children to wrath, lest they should become discouraged. The mother, too, though we have no precise knowledge of her, must have been imbued with those lofty ideas of
which we catch a trace in the mothers of Samuel, John the
Baptist, and Jesus. Perhaps she died in his early childhood;
or her son would not in after years have so lovingly turned to
the mother of Rufus for motherhood (Rom. 16:13).

The Hebrew tongue was probably the ordinary speech of
that home. This may in a measure account for the apostle's
intimate acquaintance with the Hebrew Scriptures, which he

so often quotes. It was in Hebrew that Jesus spoke to him on the road to Damascus, and in Hebrew that he addressed the crowds from the steps of the castle. To him Jerusalem was more than Athens or Rome; and Abraham, David, Isaiah, than the heroes of the *Iliad*. He counted it no small thing to have as ancestors those holy patriarchs and prophets who had followed God from Ur, wrestled with the Angel at the Jabbok, and spoken to Him at Horeb, face to face. His pulse beat quick as he remembered that he belonged to the chosen race, God's firstborn, whose were the adoption, and the glory, and the covenants, and the giving of the law, and the service of God, and the promises. However much birth and wealth flaunted before his eyes, he held himself to have been born of a nobler ancestry, to belong to a higher aristocracy. From his tribe had sprung the first king of Israel, whose name he was proud to bear.

His early education was very religious. "He was a Pharisee, and the son of a Pharisee" (Acts 23:6). In our day the word Pharisee is a synonym for religious pride and hypocrisy; but we must never forget that in those old Jewish days the Pharisee represented some of the noblest traditions of the Hebrew people. Amid the prevailing indifference the Pharisees stood for a strict religious life. As against the scepticism of the Sadducees, who believed in neither spirit nor unseen world, the Pharisees held to the resurrection of the dead, and the life of the world to come.

His early home was dominated by these austere and strong religious conceptions, and the boy imbibed them. According to the straitest sect of his religion, he lived a Pharisee. He was proud that at the earliest possible moment he had been initiated into the rites and privileges of his religion, being "circumcised the eighth day." As he heard of proselytes entering the covenant of his fathers in mature life, he congratulated himself that as a child he had been admitted into covenant relationship with God.

He was blameless in outward life. As touching the righteousness which is of the law, so far as outward observances went, he was blameless. There was no precept in the moral or ceremonial law which he would consciously disregard; and though the rabbis had built upon the law of Moses an immense superstructure of casuistical comments and minute injunctions, he bravely set himself to master them. He would upon leaving market or street carefully wash his hands of any defilement contracted through touching what had been handled by the uncircumcised. He often thanked God that he was not as other men. He was taught to fast twice in the week, and give tithes of all he possessed. He would observe the Sabbath and festivals with punctilious and awful care. "Brethren," he said on one occasion, "I have lived, before God, in all conscience until this day."

His nature must have been warmhearted and fervid from the first. The tears that flowed at Miletus, the heart that was nearly broken on his last journey to Jerusalem, the pathetic appeals and allusions of his epistles, his capacity for ardent and constant friendships—were not the growth of his mature years; but were present, in germ at least, from his earliest childhood. He must always have been extremely sensitive to kindness; and the contrast between his remembrance of his friends in after life, and his entire reticence about his parents, and brothers or sisters, shows how bitter and final was that disowning which followed on his avowal of Christianity. There is more than appears on the surface in his remark, "For whom I suffered the loss of all things" (Phil. 3:8).

The zeal, which in after years led him to persecute the church, was already stirring in his heart. "I am a Jew," he once said, "born in Tarsus of Cilicia, instructed according to the strict manner of the law of our fathers, being zealous for God" (Acts 22:3). Indeed, he tells us that he advanced in the Jews' religion beyond many of his own age among his countrymen, being more exceedingly zealous for the traditions of the fathers. He did not hold truth indolently or superficially, or as a necessity of his early nurture and education; but as a tincture which had saturated and dyed the deepest emotions of a very intense nature.

The days of his childhood must have passed thus: At five he began to read the Scriptures; at six he would be sent to the school of a neighboring rabbi; at ten he would be instructed in the oral law; at thirteen he would become, by a kind of confirmation, a son of the law. Between the ages of thirteen and sixteen he would be sent to Jerusalem, to pursue his training for the office of a rabbi, to which he was evidently designated by the ambition of his father. It was easy for the boy to do thus, as he had a married sister in Jerusalem with whom he could lodge during his attendance in the classes of the illustrious Gamaliel. "I was brought up in this city," he said afterwards, "at the feet of Gamaliel."

We must not omit to record that during these boyish years he acquired a trade, which served him usefully when hard pressed for means of livelihood. Every Jew was taught a trade, generally that of his father. Probably Paul's family for generations back had been engaged in weaving a dark coarse cloth of goat's hair. From his childhood he must have been familiar with the rattle of the looms, in which the long hair of the mountain goats was woven into a strong material, suitable alike for the outer coats of artisans or for tents, and known as Cilician cloth, after the name of the province in which Tarsus was situated. This handicraft was poorly remunerated; but in Paul's case it was highly suitable to the exigencies of a wandering life. Other trades would require a settled workshop and expensive apparatus; but this was a simple industry, capable of being pursued anywhere, and needing the smallest possible apparatus and tools.

Across a gulf of fifty years from the confinement of a Roman prison, Paul had time to review these things which he had before counted gain. To the earnest gaze which he directed towards them, the receding shores of his early life came near again; and as he counted up their treasures he wrote across them—loss, dross: "the things that were gain to me, these I counted loss for Christ. Yea, doubtless, and I count all things but loss for the excellency of the knowledge of Christ Jesus my Lord" (Phil. 3:7, 8).

2

Thy Martyr Stephen

Acts 7

The method of God's introduction of His greatest servants to the world differs widely. In some cases they rise gradually and majestically, like the dawn. In other cases they flash like the lightning on the dark abyss of night. Sometimes God charges a man with a message, and launches him forth suddenly and irresistibly. Such a man was Elijah, with his "Thus saith the Lord, before whom I stand." And such was Stephen.

We know little or nothing of his antecedents. That he was a Hellenist Jew is almost certain; and that he had personally known and consorted with the Son of Man, whom he afterwards recognized in His glory, is more than probable. But of father, mother, birthplace, and education, we know nothing. We have the story of one day, the record of one speech—that day his last, that speech his apology and defense for his life.

Three streams of thought were meeting in tumultuous eddies in Jerusalem.

There were *the Jews of the Pharisee party*, represented by Gamaliel, Saul of Tarsus, and other notable men. They were characterized by an intense religiousness, which circled around their ancestry, their initial rite, their law, their temple. Were they not Abraham's children? Had not God entered into special covenant relations with them, of which circumcision was the outward sign and seal? Were they not zealous in their observance of the law, which had been uttered amid the thunderpeals of Sinai, not for themselves alone, but for the world?

Next came the *Hebrew Christian Church*, led and represented by the Apostles. To culture and eloquence they laid no claim. Of founding a new religious organization they had no idea. That they should ever live to see Judaism superseded by the teaching they were giving, or Christianity existing apart from the system in which they had been nurtured, was a thought which, in the furthest flights of their imagination, never occurred to them. Their Master had rigorously observed the Jewish rights and feasts; and they followed in his steps, and impressed a similar course of action on their adherents. And it seems certain that, if nothing had happened of the nature of Stephen's apology and protests, the church would have become another Jewish sect, distinguished by the piety and purity of its adherents, and by their strange belief in the Messiahship of Jesus of Nazareth, who had been crucified under Pontius Pilate.

Lastly, there were *the converts from among the Hellenist Jews*. In Acts 6:1, these are distinctly referred to; and in verse 9 the various synagogues in which they were wont to meet are enumerated—of these Stephen was the holy and eloquent exponent.

The origin of the Hellenist or Grecian Jews must be traced back to the captivity, which God overruled to promote the dissemination of Jewish conceptions through the world. It was but a small contingent that returned to Jerusalem with Nehemiah and Ezra; the vast majority elected to remain in the land of their adoption for purposes of trade. They slowly spread thence throughout Asia Minor to the cities of its seaboard and the highland districts of its interior, planting everywhere the synagogue, with its protest on behalf of the unity and the spirituality of God. But their free contact with the populace of many lands wrought a remarkable change on them.

While the Jews of Jerusalem and Judea shrank from the defiling touch of heathenism, and built higher the wall of separation, growing continually prouder, more bitter, more narrow, the Jews that were scattered through the world became more liberal and cosmopolitan. They dropped their Hebrew mother tongue for Greek; they read the Septuagint version of the Scriptures; their children were influenced by Greek culture and philosophy; they became able to appreciate the purposes of God moving through the channels of universal history; they learned that though their fathers had received the holy oracles for mankind, yet God had nowhere left Himself without witness. Many of these open-minded Hellenist Jews, when they had passed the meridian of their days in successful trade, came back and settled in Jerusalem. The different countries from which they hailed were represented by special synagogues: one of the Libertines who had been freed from slavery, one of the Cyrenians, one of the Alexandrians, one of them of Cilicia and of Asia. The mention of the latter is specially interesting when we recall that the chief city of Cilicia was Tarsus.

After some years of absence, Paul returned to settle at Jerusalem. It is possible that its Jewish leaders, having been impressed by his remarkable talents and enthusiastic devotion to Judaism, had summoned him to take part in, or lead, that opposition to Christianity, to which events were daily more irrevocably committing them. It is almost certain, also, that to facilitate his operations he was at this time nominated to a seat in the Sanhedrin, which enabled him to give his vote against the followers of Jesus (Acts 26:10).

His first impressions about the followers of "the Way," as the early disciples were termed, were wholly unfavorable. It seemed to him sheer madness to suppose that the crucified Nazarene could be the long-looked-for Messiah, or that He had risen from the dead. He, therefore, threw himself into the breach, and took the lead in disputing with Stephen, who had just been raised to office in the nascent church; and, not content with the conservative and timid attitude which the Apostles had preserved for some five years, was now leading an aggressive and forward policy.

Can we not imagine those eager disputings in the Cilician

synagogue between these two ardent and vehement spirits, close akin at heart, as the future would show, though now apparently so far divided. Each thoroughly versed in Scripture, each agile in argument and strong of soul, each devoted to the holy traditions of the past; but the one blinded by an impenetrable veil, while to the other heaven was open, and the Son of Man was revealed standing at the right hand of God.

Like most who speak God's truth for the first time, Stephen was greatly misunderstood. We gather this from the charges made against him by the false witnesses, whom the Sanhedrin suborned. They accused him of uttering blasphemous words against Moses, of speaking against the Temple and the law, of declaring that Jesus of Nazareth would destroy the Temple, and change customs delivered by Moses. And as we attentively follow his argument, we can see how it was that these impressions had been caused.

Saul would expatiate on the glories of the Temple, standing on the site where for centuries Jehovah had been worshipped. But Stephen would insist that any holy soul might worship God in the temple of his own soul; that there was no temple in the old time when God spake to Abraham and the patriarchs; that David was discouraged from building one; and that at the time of its dedication Solomon expressly acknowledged that God did not dwell in temples made with hands.

Saul would insist on the necessity of the rite of circumcision. But Stephen would argue that it could not be all-important, since God made promises to Abraham long before that rite was instituted.

Saul would show the unlikelihood of Jesus being God's Deliverer, because He was not recognized by the leaders and shepherds of Israel. Stephen would rejoin that there was nothing extraordinary in this, since Joseph had been sold for jealousy, and Moses rejected on three distinct occasions, "Which of the prophets did not your fathers persecute?" (v. 52).

Saul said that all the prophets pointed to the glorious advent of the Messiah. Stephen reviewed Moses, the Prophets, and the

Psalms, and showed that it behoved the Christ to suffer.

Saul affirmed that nothing could supersede Moses. Stephen quoted Moses himself as asserting that the Lord God would raise up a greater prophet than himself.

All this Stephen affirmed with the greatest reverence and awe. He spoke of the God of Glory; of the great one of the past as "our fathers"; of the angel that spake at Sinai; and the living oracles of Scripture. And yet it is undeniable that he saw with undimmed vision that Jesus of Nazareth must change the customs which Moses delivered, and lead His church into more spiritual aspects of truth.

How little he weened that he was dropping seed-germs into the heart of his chief opponent that were to bear harvests to one hundredfold—nay, to many millions-fold, through the centuries, and in the broad harvest field of the world! Thus a plant may yield one white flower, but the seeds it drops may live and bloom again in uncounted springs.

We know little of *Stephen's life.* It was more than probable that he knew Jesus in His earthly life, for he instantly recognized Him in the heavenly vision. Perhaps he had followed Him during the latter part of His ministry. Surely he must have seen Him die; for the traits of His dying beauty molded his own last hours. How meekly to bear his cross; to plead for his murderers with a divine charity; to breathe his departing spirit into unseen hands; to find in death the gate of life, and amid the horror of a public execution the secret of calm and peace—all these were rays of light caught from the Cross where his Master had poured out His soul unto death.

This, too, powerfully affected Paul. That light on the martyr's face; that evident glimpse into the unseen Holy; those words; that patience and forgiveness; that peace which enwrapt his mangled body, crushed and bleeding, as he fell asleep—he could never forget them. Long years after, when a similar scene of hate was environing himself, he reverted to Christ's martyr, Stephen, and counted it a high honor meekly to follow in his steps.

3

A Light From Heaven

Acts 9

If the importance of events can be estimated by the amount of space given in Scripture to their narration, the arrest placed by the risen Lord upon the career of Saul of Tarsus must take the second place in the story of the New Testament. It is described three times, with great minuteness of detail—first by Luke, and twice by himself—and the narration occupies more space than the story of any other event except the crucifixion of our Lord.

It was one of the deepest convictions of the Apostle in all his after life that he had veritably and certainly seen the Lord; and was therefore as really empowered to be a witness of His resurrection as any who had companied with Him, beginning from the baptism of John until the day that He was received up. "Am I not an Apostle? Have I not seen Jesus our Lord?" he asks (1 Cor. 9:1). And after enumerating the Lord's appearances after His resurrection, he adds, placing that scene on the road to Damascus on a level with the rest, "Last of all, as unto one born out of due time, He appeared to me also" (15:8).

Six days before, Saul had left Jerusalem with a small retinue furnished as his escort by the high priest. The journey was long and lonely, giving time for reflection, of which he had known but little during the crowding events of the previous months. He had been too closely occupied by those domiciliary visits, those constant trials, those scourgings, tortures, and martyrdoms; and in the incessant occupation he had been drifting with the rush of events, without taking his bearings or realizing their precise direction.

It was high noon. Unlike most travelers, he forbore to spend even an hour in the retirement of his tent for shelter from the downward rays of the sun, piercing like swords, while all the air was breathless with the heat. He was too weary of his own musings, too eager to be at his work. Suddenly the little cavalcade left the stony wastes over which the track had lain, and began to pass beneath "the flickering shadow of ancient olives," while Damascus suddenly came into view, amid a soft haze of verdure: its gardens, orchards, and groves making an emerald setting for its terraced roofs and white glistening cupolas.

The goal of the long journey was well in sight. Within an hour or two he would be within the gates and traversing the street called Straight, to deliver his commission to the authorities and to ascertain the best point for commencing proceedings. But suddenly a great light—above the brightness of the Syrian noontide sun—shone around him; and a voice, amid the blaze, unintelligible and inarticulate to his companions, though clear enough to himself, was heard, speaking in the familiar Aramaic, and calling him by name (Acts 26:14).

There can be no doubt, in the light of the passages we have noticed, as to the origin of that light—it came straight from the face of the glorified Savior. With some such light as this it had become illumined on the Mount of Transfiguration, when His face did shine as the sun, and His garments grew white as the light, and all the snows around reflected the golden sheen. Something of the same beauty and splendor was described by John in after years, when he tells of the vision given him in Patmos; but even this must have fallen far behind the Master's actual appearance on the way to Damascus. In the one case His countenance was as when the sun shineth in his strength; in the other its glory was above the brightness of the sun.

In the light of that moment the Apostle saw many things.

In the glory of that light he became convinced of the truth of Christianity. His objection to Christianity was not that Jesus of Nazareth had been crucified. Had this been all, the young Pharisee would have respected Him. His blameless life; His teaching of the spirituality and unity of the Divine Nature; His belief in the resurrection of the dead; His fearless exposure of what was false and vicious, would even have attracted His admiration. But it was intolerable that He should pose as the Messiah, or that His followers should charge the rulers with the murder of the long-expected King.

There was only one thing that could convince him. He must see this Jesus of Nazareth, whom he knew to have been crucified, living on the other side of death; he must be able to recognize and establish His identity; he must hear Him speak. Such evidence given to himself would be conclusive; but nothing less would avail. If from heaven the Man of Nazareth and the Cross were to speak to him, radiant with light, exerting Divine power—his objections would be scattered, and with another of His followers he would be compelled to cry, "My Lord and my God!"

But this very revelation was made to him. It could not be a dream, a vision, an hallucination. He was too sane to base the entire change of his career upon anything so flimsy; and in his writings he always distinguishes between these and that appearance of the Lord on the road to Damascus. No, as Barnabas said afterwards, by way of explanation to the Apostles, "he saw the Lord in the way, and the Lord spoke to him" (v. 27). He felt instantly that life must have henceforward a new meaning and purpose, and he must live to establish the faith of which he had made such determined havoc.

In the glory of that light he beheld the supreme revelation of God. Nature had told something of God. From the first, God had not left Himself without witness, in that He did good, and gave rains from heaven and fruitful seasons, filling men's hearts with food and gladness. The heavens had told His glory, and the firmament shown His handiwork. But *this* light was above the brightness of the sun, and made all

Nature's wonders pale, as stars at the dawn.

The Real Nature of Saul's War Against Christianity
The earliest name of the new sect, as we have seen, was *the Way*. In after years the Apostle was proud to adopt and use it: "I confess unto thee, that after the Way, which they call a sect, so serve I the God of our fathers" (Acts 24:14).

The young man Saul was exceedingly mad against the pilgrims of the Way. He made havoc of them, and the word is that which would be used of wild boars uprooting tender vines. He devastated them with the fury of an invading army. Not content with attacks on their public meetings, he paid visits to their homes, dragging forth the patient, holy women as well as the uncomplaining men, scourging them, thrusting them in prison, putting them to death, and compelling them to blaspheme the holy Name by which they were called.

But, like the Roman soldier who crucified the Lord, he knew not what he did. "I was a blasphemer, and a persecutor, and injurious; howbeit I obtained mercy, because I did it ignorantly in unbelief" (I Tim. 1:13).

As, however, that light fell upon his path, he suddenly awoke to discover that, instead of serving God, he was in collision with Him, and was actually uprooting and ravaging that for which the Son of his love had expended tears and blood. In persecuting the sect of the Nazarenes he was persecuting the Son of God. By every blow he struck at the infant church, he was lacerating those hands and piercing that side. By every sigh and groan extorted from the members of the Body he had elicited from the Head in heaven the remonstrance, "Saul! Saul! why persecutest thou Me?" Ah! it is an awful discovery when a great light from heaven shows a man that what he has regarded his solemn duty has been one long sin against the dearest purposes of God.

The Inadequacy of His Religion
He had lived out all that he thought to be right. So far as he

knew what religion prescribed, he was blameless. But of late he had been compelled to confess to a dull sense of uneasiness and dissatisfaction.

Two causes further instigated this uneasiness. First, he felt that his religion did not satisfy him; it gave him no such tender views of the love of God as had impressed Moses or Daniel, and it seemed ineffective to curb the imperious demands of sin.

Then it seemed as though these humble disciples of Jesus of Nazareth had something better. The meekness with which they bore their sufferings was far removed from obstinacy; the purity of their home life vindicated their professions; the light that shone upon their dying faces; the prayers for their persecutors, which they offered with their dying breath, evidenced the possession of a secret of which he knew that he was destitute.

The Source of His Uneasiness

Hitherto he may have attributed it to a morbid and melancholic element in his constitution, to the reaction of his mind from the sight of suffering, to a weakness of which he ought to rid himself as speedily as possible. He now saw that these strivings were the prickings of the great Husbandman's goad, by which He had long been attempting to bring him into that attitude, and lead him to undertake that lifework which had been prepared for him from the foundation of the world.

It was a new conception of the religious life. Henceforth he was not to do his own prompting, but God's; not to be clothed in his own righteousness, but in God's; not to cut up and destroy, but to construct; not to oppose the Nazarene, but to take His yoke, to bear His burden, to do His will.

The Course of His Future Life

Henceforth he was to be a minister and a witness of those things which he had seen, and of those in which Christ would still appear to him. All that was required of him was to live in unbroken accord with the risen Savior, beholding His beauty, inquiring in His temple, receiving His messages for transmission to others.

It was enough. He meekly asked what he must do; what the new and rightful Master of his life would have him *do*. And in answer, he was told to take the next step, which lay just before him, and suffer himself to be led into the city. He little weened how great things he would have to *suffer* (Acts 9:16). These were a secret which Christ whispered in the ear of His friend, Ananias. It would be enough for the new convert to learn it afterwards. After all, men do as much by suffering as by active toil; and the world owes as much to the anguish of its martyrs as to the words and deeds of its apologists and workers.

And then there arose before him in a flash on the high road, and in fuller development during the three days' retirement in the house of Judas, the Lord's ideal of his life— that he should be sent to Jew and Gentile; that by his simple witness he would be used to open blind eyes; that men might turn from darkness to light, from the power of Satan unto God, so as to receive remission of sin and inheritance among the sanctified.

How could he be other than obedient to the heavenly vision that summoned him to a life of self-sacrificing toil? As a token of his meek submission, he allowed them to lead him by the hand into the city, which he had expected to enter as an inquisitor; and bent low to receive instruction from one of those simple-hearted believers, whom he had expected to drag captive to Jerusalem. Such are the triumphs of the grace of God, and in His care it was shown to be exceedingly abundant.

4

The Inner Revelation of Christ

Acts 9

How different to his anticipation was Saul's entrance into
Damascus! He had probably often solaced himself during his
weary six-days' journey by picturing the reception which
would be accorded to him by the authorities at Damascus, on
his arrival at their city as the Commissioner of the High
Priest, charged with the extirpation of the Nazarene heresy.
But instead of honor, there was consternation and surprise.
No one could quite explain or understand what had taken
place. Dismounted from his horse, he went afoot; instead of
the haughty bearing of the Inquisitor, the helplessness of a
sightless man appealed for hands to lead him; shrinking
from notice and welcome, he was only too eager to reach a
lonely chamber, where he might recover from the awful effects of that collision between his mortal and sinful nature
and the holy, glorious Son of God, whom he had so
ruthlessly persecuted.

At this formative period of his life three effective agencies
were brought to bear on him.

The Work of God on His Heart

"It pleased God to reveal His Son in me" (Gal. 1:15, 16). The
Apostle knew too much of the Divine life to admit that the
vast change in him could be entirely accounted for by what
he had seen with his mortal, and now blinded eyes. He was
aware that a true and lasting work can only be achieved

when the inner eye has perceived things that are hidden from mortal sense. In other words, God, who commanded the light to shine out of darkness, must shine *in the heart* to give the light of the knowledge of his glory in the face of Jesus.

Imagine the abundance of revelations made to the blinded man during those three days and nights of silence and solitude in the house of Judas. Is it not wonderful that he became oblivious to the needs of the body, and did neither eat nor drink? There are hours when we lose all consciousness of earth, and already live in the heavenlies; when the soul loses count of the moments, sets sail from the coastline of earth, and finds itself out on the broad bosom of the ocean of eternity. Such was the experience of this soul.

During those wondrous hours God unveiled secrets which had been kept in silence through times eternal, but were manifested to him according to the commandment of the eternal God, that he might make them known unto all nations, unto obedience of faith.

But more than all was the unveiling of the indwelling Christ, living literally within him by His Spirit, so that while he was in Christ, Christ was also in him, as the branch has its place in the vine, and the vine lives through the branch.

Contact with Ananias
It is permitted to holy and humble natures greatly to help the spirit which is on the point of emerging from bondage. The little maiden, awakening from her death swoon, required food; Lazarus, whom Jesus had summoned back to life, needed to be unswathed and loosed. The offices which one can perform for another are beautifully illustrated in that simple-hearted saint, Ananias, whom the Lord at this moment called upon the scene, and to whom He entrusted the keys of the kingdom, that he might unlock Saul's way into perfect peace.

We know very little of Ananias, except that he was a devout man according to the law and was well reported of by the

Jews, but evidently he was on intimate terms with his Master; and the Lord was willing to enter into explanations and reassurances with him, before sending him forth.

He gave him a brother's welcome. Though he was fully acquainted with the object of Saul's visit to the city, he accosted him with the sweet and generous term, Brother, *Brother* Saul. What a thrill that address sent through the heart of the new convert! Pharisaism had never spoken thus; and as he became conscious of the presence of this new brother standing beside him and laying his hand on his fevered brow, the human love was the sign and symbol of the Divine.

He communicated priceless blessings; for, first, beneath the laying on of his hands, sight came clear to eyes which had beheld nothing since they had been smitten by the glory of "that light." And the touch of this devout man, accompanied as it must have been with the upward glance of prayer and faith, was also the signal for the reception of the anointing grace of the Holy Spirit, infilling, anointing, and equipping for blessed service.

He baptized him. What a baptism must that have been! What a tidal wave of emotion must have swept over him, as he realized that he was being united with Jesus by the likeness of His death!

That baptism was his final and irreversible break with his past life, the Pharisaic party, and his persecution of the adherents of "the Way." Henceforth he was avowedly one with the followers of the Nazarene. From that moment he took up his cross, and began to follow his Master. The cross and grave of Jesus must now stand between him and all that had been—all his friends, ambitions, and opinions—while he must turn his face towards labor and travail, hunger and thirst, perils and persecutions, together with the daily deliverance unto death for Jesus' sake.

The Education of the Desert Solitudes
"Immediately I conferred not with flesh and blood; neither

went I up to Jerusalem to them which were apostles before me; but I went away into Arabia" (Gal. 1:16, 17). It is not quite clear whether he began to preach before going; probably not. He wanted to be alone, to reflect on all that he had seen; to coordinate, if possible, the new with the old, the present with the past. For this he must have uninterrupted leisure, and he hungered for the isolation and solitude of the wilderness. Men like Ananias might reassure him; the apostles of the Lord might communicate much of His teaching and wondrous ministry; the holy beauty of the life of the infant church might calm and elevate his spirit; but, above all things, he wanted to be alone with Jesus, to know Him and the power of His resurrection, the anointing which makes human teaching needless, because it teaches all things. Three years under such tuition would doubtless make him so proficient that when afterwards he met those who were of repute among the apostles they would be able to add nothing unto him.

Arabia probably stands for the Sinaitic peninsula, with its sparse population, its marked physical features, its associations with Moses, and the Exodus, and Elijah.

Probably the most important work of those years was to review the entire course of Old Testament truth from the new standpoint of vision suggested by the sufferings and death of the Messiah. There was no doubt that He had been crucified in weakness, and now lived in the power of God. But how was this consistent with the anticipations of the prophets and seers of the Old Testament, who had been understood by generations of rabbis to predict an all-victorious Prince? How eagerly he turned to all the well-known Messianic passages! What ecstasy must have thrilled him as he discovered that they were all consistent with Christ's suffering unto death as the way to enter His glory! And how greatly he must have wondered that he and all his people had been so blind to the obvious meaning of the inspired Word (2 Cor. 3).

In the light of this revelation he could better understand his own call to minister to the Gentiles, for this was one of the special provisions of the Abrahamic covenant: "In thee and in thy seed shall all the nations of the earth be blessed" (Gen. 22:18).

But deeper than all was God's work with his soul. Grain by grain his proud self-reliance and impetuosity were worn away. As it happened to Moses during the forty years of shepherd life, so it befell Saul of Tarsus. No longer confident in himself, he was henceforth more than content to be the slave of Jesus Christ, going where he was sent, doing as he was bidden, and serving as the instrument of His will. We all need to go to Arabia to learn lessons like these. The Lord Himself was led up into the wilderness. And, in one form or another, every soul which has done a great work in the world has been passed through similar periods of obscurity, suffering, disappointment, or solitude.

5

The Emergence
of the Life Purpose

Acts 9

At the moment of conversion there are two questions that arise naturally upon our lips: First, Who art Thou, Lord? and next, What wilt Thou have me to do? *As to the first,* we can only await the gradual revelation, as when the dawn slowly breaks on a widespread landscape. It will take an eternity to know all that Jesus Christ is and can be to His own. *As to the second,* we are no less dependent on the Divine revealing hand, indicating the path we are to tread, showing the scheme which the Divine mind has conceived.

Often at the beginning of the new life we attempt to forecast the work which we hope to accomplish. We take into account our tastes and aptitudes, our faculties and talents, our birth and circumstances. From these we infer that we shall probably succeed best along a certain line of useful activity. But as the moments lengthen into years, it becomes apparent that the door of opportunity is closing in that direction. It is a bitter disappointment. We refuse to believe that the hindrances to the fulfilment of our cherished hopes can be permanent. Patience, we cry, will conquer every difficulty. The entrance may be strait, but surely it is passable. At last we shall reach the wide and large place of successful achievement. We cast ourselves against the closing door, as sea birds on the illuminated glass of the lighthouse tower, to fall dazed and bewildered to the ground. And it is only after such a period of disappointment that we come to perceive that God's ways are not as our ways, nor His thoughts as our thoughts; and that He has other work for us to do, for which He has been preparing us, though we knew it not. When we are young we gird ourselves, and attempt to walk whither we will; but in after years we are guided by another, and taken whither we would not.

There is a marvelously apposite illustration of these facts of common experience in the life story which we are considering. Without doubt, at the beginning of his Christian career, the Apostle felt strongly drawn to minister to his own people. He was a Hebrew, and the son of Hebrews. The pure blood of the chosen race flowed through his heart, nourishing it with the great memories of the past. What was the meaning of his having been cradled and nourished in the heart of Judaism, except that he might better understand and win Jews? Did not his training in the strictest sect of their religion, and at the feet of Gamaliel, give him a special claim on those who held "that jewel of the law" in special reverence and honor?

But he was destined to discover that his new-found Master had other purposes for his life, and that he had been specially prepared and called to preach *among the Gentiles* the unsearchable riches of Christ, and make *all men* see the fellowship of the mystery which from all generations had been hid in God.

During his sojourn in the Sinaitic peninsula we may well believe that his soul turned towards his people with ardent desire. Surely it would not be difficult to unfold the meaning of the sacred symbolism through which their forefathers had been disciplined in those very wastes. That the rock was Christ; that the water which flowed over the sands foreshadowed His mission to the world; that the law given from Sinai had been fulfilled and reedited in the holy life of

Jesus of Nazareth—to teach all this, and much more, and to lead his people from the desert wastes of Pharisaism to the heavenly places of which Canaan was the type, was the hope and longing of his heart. What work could be more congenial to his tastes and attitudes than this?

On his return to Damascus he at once commenced his crusade in the synagogues. "Straightway," we are told, "he preached Christ in the synagogues, that He is the Son of God. And all that heard him were amazed" (vv. 20, 21). How encouraged he was by these early successes! How evidently God seemed to be setting His seal and imprimatur on his decisions! Visions of national repentance and conversion passed across his eager soul, and he dared to hope that he should live to see the dry bones become a great army for God.

But the vision was soon overcast. So violent was the hatred with which he was regarded by his fellow countrymen, that he was in imminent danger of his life.

Still, however, his purpose was unchanged. He went up to Jerusalem with the intention of seeing Peter. But in this he would probably have failed had it not been for the intervention of Barnabas, who, according to an old tradition, had been his fellow student, educated with himself at the feet of Gamaliel. Through his good offices he was brought into contact with Peter and James, and was, not improbably, received into the house of Mary, the mother of Mark, and sister to the good Cypriote (Col. 4:10). A blessed fortnight followed. He was with them, coming in and going out at Jerusalem, and especially engaged in holy and loving fellowship with Peter, the acknowledged leader of the Church.

What Peter could not tell him, James could. For he had shared the home of Nazareth, but had remained unbelieving till the Resurrection convinced him. He would recount the story of the early years, and corroborate Peter's narrative of events from the Easter dawn to the Day of Pentecost.

But Saul had other business in those happy days. He seems to have avoided the churches of Judea which were in

Christ, and to have again sought the synagogues. "He spake and disputed against the Grecian Jews." But here also his efforts were met by rebuffs: "They went about to slay him" (v. 29).

Yet in spite of coldness and antipathy, he clung tenaciously to his cherished purpose. "Surely," he cried, "it cannot be that Jerusalem will refuse my words! She has such ample proof of my sincerity, she must be willing at least to listen to the arguments which I have found so imperative; surely my marvelous change must arrest and impress her. Let me stay. To transfer me elsewhere would be a serious waste of power. I shall do better work here among people who know me so well, and conditions I can understand, than would be possible anywhere else in the world."

In a similar manner we have all cherished our life-purposes. We have forecasted our future, as liable to lie in a certain direction, and have dearly desired that it should do so. Not till long years have passed have we realized that the Lord's plan was so much wiser and grander than our own.

The Closing Door

It began to close at Damascus; it closed still further when persecution arose at Jerusalem: but the final act was as Saul was praying in the Temple.

It would appear that he had gone there to be alone, away from the many voices that were endeavoring to counsel him. For though he had been but a few days in the city, antipathy against him had already risen to such a height that his life was in danger; and it was necessary to consider seriously what to do—should he stay, or go? The babble of voices confused him, deafening the whisper of the still, small voice; his attention was too distracted by human suggestions to be perfectly open to the directing finger of God. So he betook himself to the Temple, where his Master had so often been. And, as he knelt in prayer in some quiet spot, he saw Him, whom his soul loved and sought. And the risen Lord gave clear and unmistakable directions, as He always will to those who can say with the Psalmist: "My soul is silent to the Lord, for my expectation is from Him" (Ps. 62:5). "I saw Him saying unto me, Make haste, and get thee quickly out of Jerusalem; because they will not receive of the testimony concerning Me."

It is easy to explain why they would not accept his testimony. There was too much of the Cross in it. It was sufficiently mortifying to their pride to learn that the son of the carpenter was the long-anticipated Messiah; but to be told further that the true life could only be entered by union with that supreme act of self-renunciation was intolerable. This side of Christianity is now too little appreciated, and so the offense of the Cross has largely ceased. But wherever it is consistently advocated and practiced, it is certain to arouse the sharpest controversy.

Saul, as we have seen, did not willingly accept this as the ultimatum, and still argued that Jerusalem would afford the most suitable sphere for his ministry. But all debate was at last summarily closed by the words, "Depart, for I will send thee far hence to the Gentiles."

The Opened Door

So the disciples brought the hunted preacher down to Caesarea, and sent him forth to Tarsus; and not improbably he resumed his tent making there, content to await the Lord's will and bidding. But the years passed slowly. Possibly four or five were spent in comparative obscurity and neglect. That he wrought for Christ in the immediate vicinity of his home is almost certain, as we shall see; but the word of the Lord awaited fulfilment.

At last one day, as he waited, he heard a voice saying in the doorway, "Does Saul live here?" And in another moment the familiar face of his old college-friend was peering in on him, with a glad smile of recognition. Then the story was told of the marvelous outbreak of God's work in Antioch, of the overflowing blessing and the breaking nets, and Barnabas pleaded with him to return to help him gather in the whitening harvest of the first great Gentile city which the Gospel had moved. "And he brought him to Antioch; and it came to pass that a whole year they assembled themselves with the church and taught much people" (Acts 11:26).

6

The Apostle of the Gentiles

Acts 11

It is probable that during his years of quiet work in Cilicia and Syria, Saul of Tarsus was being led with increasing clearness to apprehend God's purpose in his life—that he should be the Apostle of the Gentiles. Up till now Judaism had been the only door into Christianity; henceforth the door of faith was to stand wide open to Gentiles also, without circumcision. But still the true channel bed of his life was hardly discovered until circumstances transpired which will now demand our notice.

Summoned to Antioch

Halfway through Luke's narrative the center of interest shifts from the mother-church at Jerusalem to one which had been founded shortly before the time we are describing, in the gay, frivolous, busy, beautiful city of Antioch. Antioch was an emporium of trade, a meeting place for the Old World and the New, "an Oriental Rome, in which all the forms of the civilized life of the empire found some representation." It is for ever famous in Christian annals, because a number of unordained and unnamed disciples, fleeing from Jerusalem in the face of Saul's persecution, dared to preach the Gospel to Greeks, and to gather the converts into a church, in entire disregard of the initial rite of Judaism. There, also, the disciples of "the Way" were first called Christians from the holy name which was constantly on the lips of teachers and taught.

The population of Antioch was a rabble of all races; but the Greek element predominated, with its licentious rites, its vivacious, sparkling intellect, its marvelously elegant and subtle tongue, its passion for the theatre, the arena, and the racecourse. There was need indeed that the river of Life should find its way into that swamp of beautiful but deadly corruption; but probably none of the leaders of the church would have dared to take the initial step of conducting its streams thither. Peter and the church at Jerusalem were only just learning, through amazing incidents in the house of Cornelius, that God was prepared to grant to Gentile proselytes repentance unto life. It was left, therefore, to a handful of fugitive, Hellenistic Jews, men of Cyprus and Cyrene, to break through the barriers of the centuries, and begin preaching the Lord Jesus to the Greeks at Antioch. Instantly the Divine Spirit honored their word, gave testimony to the word of God's grace, and a great number believed and turned to the Lord (Acts 11:19-21).

As soon as tidings of these novel proceedings reached Jerusalem, the church dispatched Barnabas, who was himself a Cypriote, to make inquiries and report. His verdict was definite and reassuring. He had no hesitation in affirming that it was definite work of God's grace; he rejoiced that these simple souls had been thrust into so ripe and plentiful a harvest; and he carried on the work which had been inaugurated with such success that "much people was added unto the Lord" (v. 21).

His success, however, only added to the perplexity and difficulty of the situation, and he found himself face to face with a great problem. The Gentiles were pressing into the church, and taking their places on an equality with Jews at the Supper and Love feasts, an action which the more conservative Jews greatly resented. The single-hearted man was hardly able to cope with the problem. But he remembered that at his conversion his old friend and fellow student had been specially commissioned to preach to the Gentiles; and hoping that he might be ready with a solution, he departed to Tarsus to seek Saul, and having found him he brought him to Antioch.

But this year's experience at Antioch was of the utmost consequence to Saul. He learned from Barnabas the conclusion to which the church at Jerusalem had come, on hearing Peter's recital of God's dealings with Cornelius and his household (Acts 11:18); he noticed how evidently the Spirit of God set His seal upon appeals, whether by himself or others, addressed directly to the Gentiles, and thus was led with that deep appreciation which comes from the education of circumstances to see that believing Gentiles were fellow-members of the church and fellow heirs of the promises.

We need not stay over his brief visit to Jerusalem at the end of his year's ministry at Antioch, to carry alms from the Gentile Christians to their suffering Jewish brethren. Suffice it to say that it established a precedent which he followed in after life, and proved that there was no sort of antagonism between the new society and the old, but that all were one in Christ.

Set Apart by the Holy Spirit
It was a momentous hour in the history of the church when, on the return of Barnabas and Paul from Jerusalem, they met, with three others, for a season of fasting and prayer. What was the immediate reason for this special session we cannot say; but it is significant that the three prophets and two teachers represented between them five different countries. Were they yearning after their own people, and wistful to offer them the Gospel, as they now saw they might offer it, apart from the trammels and restraints of Judaism? We cannot tell. That, however, was the birth-hour of modern missions. The Holy Ghost, Christ's Vicar, the Director and Administrator of the church, bade the little group set apart two out of their number to a mission which He would unfold to

them, as they dared to step out in obedience to His command.

There was no hesitation or delay. The church set them free from their duties, and the Holy Spirit sent them forth. And that journey was a complete answer to all the questions by which they had been perplexed.

In Cyprus, to which they were first attracted, because Barnabas was connected with it through his birth and estate, though they proclaimed the word of God from one end to the other in the synagogues of the Jews, they had no fruit till the Roman governor called them before him, and sought to hear their message, on hearing which he believed.

After landing on the mainland, Paul, contrary to the judgment of John Mark, struck up from the seacoast to the far-reaching tablelands of the interior, four thousand feet above the sea level, with the evident intention of establishing churches on the great trade route which ran through Asia Minor from Tarsus to Ephesus. What might not be the result for East and West, if this great mutual bridge were to become a highway for the feet of the Son of God! But there the same experience awaited him.

The Jews in Antioch and Pisidia refused, while the Gentiles welcomed them. Indeed he was compelled to turn publicly from his own countrymen, and hold up the Gospel as light and salvation to those whom the prophet described as at the uttermost end of the earth. Then it was that the word of the Lord spread throughout all the region.

Everywhere it was the Jewish element that was obstructive and implacable; while the Gentiles, when left to themselves, received them and their message with open arms. God gave manifest testimony to the word of His grace whenever they unfolded it to the Gentiles; set before those eager seekers the open door of faith; and granted signs and wonders to be wrought of His servants' hands (Acts 14:3, 27; 15:12).

As Paul quietly studied these indications of God's will, he needed no angel to tell him that as Israel would not hear, God was provoking them to jealousy by them who were not a people. He saw that the original branches were being broken off, that the wild olive grafts might take their place.

His Apostolate Recognized by the Apostles

In the course of several interviews it became increasingly evident to James, Peter, and John, that their former persecutor had received a Divine commission to the Gentiles. They realized that he had been entrusted with the Gospel of the uncircumcision. Peter especially recognized that he who wrought in himself unto the apostolate of the Jew was equally energetic in this fervid soul unto the Gentile. The responsible leaders of the mother church could not help perceiving the grace that was given to him; and finally they gave to him the right hand of fellowship, that he should go to the Gentiles, while they went to the circumcision.

This was the further and final confirmation of the purpose which had been forming in his heart; and he recognized that he was appointed an herald and an apostle, a teacher of the Gentiles in faith and truth. He gloried in this ministry, and often spoke of the grace which had been given to him, the least of all saints, to preach unto the Gentiles the unsearchable riches of Christ. He never failed to begin his work in any place by an honest endeavor to save some of his own flesh; but he always realized that his supreme stewardship was to those who were called uncircumcision by that which was called circumcision in the flesh made by hands.

7

Fourteen Years Ago

II Corinthians 12

If we count back fourteen years from the writings of II Corinthians, we shall find ourselves amid the events narrated the thirteenth and fourteenth chapters of the Book of the Acts; especially at that momentous hour in the history of Christianity when five men, representing five different countries, met together to fast and pray about the state of the world and their duty in respect to it. The Evangelist tells us in two chapters the results of that conference, in the separation and sending forth of the two missionaries; and of the hardships, difficulties, and sufferings through which they fulfilled their high calling. But Paul draws aside the veil from his heart and shows us what his inner experiences were during those wonderful months. He was a man in Christ, caught up into Paradise, the third heaven, to hear unspeakable words.

Perhaps even Barnabas, who shared the toils and perils of this man of God, had little or no conception of what his companion was experiencing. He beheld the same scenes on which their outward gaze rested, but not the visions that were unfolded to the inner eye. He heard the voices that sounded in their ears, of blaspheming and reviling critics, with which so few notes of comfort and encouragement blended; but he was not aware of the still small voice of Christ, which bade Paul have no fear.

The Apostle's Description

"A man in Christ." He was in Christ, but that did not make him less a man. There are three qualities in a truly manly character:

Resolution—that a man will take up one high ambition and aim. It was his persistent ambition to preach the Gospel where Christ had not been named, so that they should see to whom no tidings of Him had come, and they who had not heard should understand.

Fortitude—that a man should be able to sustain sorrow and heartrending anguish. Every true man needs this, for there is no one without his hours of heartrending grief, when it seems as though the heartstrings must break and the life-blood be shed. Then to be strong, to steer straight onward, to dare to praise God, to sit alone and keep silence, because He hath laid it upon us, to put our mouths in the dust, if so be there may be hope—here is fortitude indeed. But Paul manifested this also, when he bore with uncomplaining nobility the cowardice of Mark, the relentless hatred of his fellow-countrymen, and after his stoning at Lystra, aroused from what had seemed to be his death swoon, struggled back into the city from which he had been dragged to all appearance a corpse, and having saluted the brethren, and specially the young Timothy, started on the following morning to continue his loved work in the neighboring cities of Lycaonia.

Courage—Paul never lacked courage. He never flinched from facing an amphitheatre full of raging fanatics, or braving consuls and procurators, or from withstanding an Apostle who deserved to be blamed. And his heroic courage was conspicuously manifested in this very journey, that instead of taking an easier and direct route home by way of his native city and the Cilician Gates, he dared to retrace his steps to each of the cities in which he had preached, confirming the souls of the disciples, exhorting them to continue in the faith, and that through many tribulations we must enter into the kingdom of God. At great personal risk he stayed long enough in each place to appoint elders in the infant communities, and to pray with fasting, commending them to God, on whom they believed.

To Such, Bridal Moments Come

Days of the bridal of heaven and earth—high days—hours of vision and ecstasy—when the tide runs high and fast, and the cup of life brims to overflow. "I knew such an one caught up even to the third heaven, to Paradise, and heard unspeakable words, which it is not lawful for a man to utter. On behalf of such a man will I glory" (vv. 2, 4, 5).

Such experiences may come in hours of great pain. The conjecture has been hazarded that this rapture into Paradise took place during the Apostle's stoning at Lystra. But be this as it may, he could find no words to tell what he saw and heard. Paradise were indeed a poor place if words could describe it. The third heaven were not worthy of its Maker if its glories did not transcend our furthest imaginings. He hath set eternity in our heart, a capacity for the infinite, a yearning after the Divine. Translate into words for me the sighings of the wind through the forest, and the withdrawal of the sea down a pebbly beach, and the spring sunlight playing on the hyacinth-strewn grass. You cannot! Then you know why the Apostle described his experiences in Paradise as unspeakable.

Do not expect the vision of Paradise to linger; it would dazzle you, and make life unnatural and unreal. Do not regret the passage of the blessed, rapturous hours, light of step and fleet of pace. Do not think that you have fallen from grace when their flush and glow are over. Whether they fall to your constant lot or not, or even if they never visit you, you are still in Christ, still joined to the Lord, still accepted in the Beloved; and neither height of rapture nor depth of depression shall ever separate you from the love of God, which is in Jesus Christ our Lord. Be content, then, to turn, as Jesus did, from the rapture of Paradise, presented on the Transfigura-

tion Mount, to take the way of the cross, through which you
will become able to open Paradise to souls in despair, like the
dying thief.

The Discipline of Pain

We need not stay to discuss what was the nature of Paul's
thorn in the flesh. It is not very material now and here.
Enough that it was very painful. Paul calls it "a stake," as
though he were impaled; and it must have been physical, as
he could not have prayed thrice for the removal of a moral
taint, and been refused. In infinite wisdom God permitted
the messenger of Satan to buffet His servant; and all through
that first missionary journey he had to face a long succession
of buffetings. There were perils of robbers, of waters, of
mountain passes, and of violent crowds; but in addition to
all, there was the lacerating thorn.

He probably suffered from weak eyes, or some distressing
form of ophthalmia. We infer this from the eagerness of his
Galatian converts to give him their eyes, from his dependence on an amanuensis, and from the clumsy letters with
which he wrote the postscripts to his epistles (Gal. 6:11). And
if this were the case, the pain would be greatly aggravated as
he faced the keen blasts that swept the mountain plateau on
which the Pisidian Antioch was situated.

Was it during this journey that he besought the Lord on
three separate occasions for deliverance, and received the
assurance that though the thorns were left, more than sufficient grace would be given? If so, like a peal of bells, at
Antioch, Iconium, Derbe, and Lystra, he must have heard
the music of those tender words: My grace is sufficient, *sufficient, sufficient* for thee! Sufficient when friends forsake, and
foes pursue; sufficient to make thee strong against a raging
synagogue, or a shower of stones; sufficient for excessive
labors of body, and conflicts of soul; sufficient to enable thee
to do as much work, and even more, than if the body were
perfectly whole—for my strength is made perfect only amid
the conditions of mortal weakness.

In estimating the greatness of a man's lifework, it is fair to take into consideration the difficulties under which he has wrought. And how greatly does our appreciation of the Apostle rise when we remember that he was incessantly in pain. Instead, however, of sitting down in despair, and pleading physical infirmity as his excuse for doing nothing, he bravely claimed the grace which waited within call, and did greater work through God's enabling might than he could have done through his own had it been unhindered by his weakness.

Ah, afflicted ones, your disabilities were meant to unite with God's enablings; your weakness to mate His power. Do not sit down before that mistaken marriage, that uncongenial business, that unfortunate partnership, that physical weakness, that hesitancy of speech, that disfigurement of face, as though they must necessarily maim and conquer you. God's grace is at hand—sufficient—and at its best when human weakness is most profound. Appropriate it, and learn that those that wait on God are stronger in their weakness than the sons of men in their stoutest health and vigor.

8

A Lesson of Guidance

Acts 15

After a brief respite, Paul proposed to Barnabas that they should return to visit the brethren in every city wherein they had proclaimed the word of the Lord, and see how they fared. This was the beginning of his second missionary journey, which was to have far-reaching results.

Barnabas suggested that they should take Mark with them as before, a proposition which his companion positively refused to entertain. Mark had deserted them on the threshold of their previous expedition, and there was grave fear that he might do so again. Barnabas was as strong on the other side. Perhaps he felt that he had some rights in the matter, as the senior in age, because of the tie of blood between himself and his sister's son. At last the contention reached so acute a stage that the church became aware of it, and took Paul's side, for the narrative of the Acts tells us that when Paul chose Silas, and went forth, "he was commended by the brethren to the grace of the Lord" (v. 40).

If you are compelled to differ from your companions, let it be in love; let them feel that you have no interests to serve but those of truth. If Lot quarrels with you, it is best to give him his own terms and send him away; God will give you ever so much more than he can take. Only do nothing to drive the Holy Dove of God from your bosom. Perfect love is the only atmosphere in which the Divine Spirit can manifest His gracious help.

Through regions rich in flowers and natural beauty Paul and Silas traversed Syria and Cilicia, confirming the infant churches, which probably owed their existence to Paul's earliest efforts. So through the Cilician Gates to Tarsus, his native city. But there was no welcome for him there. After some days' toilsome journey they came to Derbe, Lystra, and Iconium, so tragically associated with the former journey.

What a welcome Paul would receive! How many inquiries would be made after Barnabas! How much to tell and hear! There was, however, a special burden on the Apostle's heart. On the occasion of his previous visit his attention had been arrested by a mere lad, who had been strongly attracted to him, watching with a lad's enthusiastic devotion his teaching, conduct, purpose, faith, longsuffering, love, and patience, and perhaps mingling with the little group that stood around him when he sank beneath the stones of those who a few days before had offered him worship. He asked for Timothy, and was glad to learn that he had not been faithless to the teachings and training of the godly women who had watched over his opening character, and instructed him in the Holy Scriptures.

He was well reported of by the brethren that were at Lystra and Iconium. The more Paul knew of him the more he was attracted to him, and finally proposed that he should accompany him on his travels as his own son in the faith. He administered the rite of circumcision, not because he deemed it obligatory, but as a matter of convenience, that there might be no obstacle to the admission of his young assistant to Jewish synagogues.

A simple ordination service was then held, in which Timothy was solemnly set apart for his great work. The elders gathered round and laid their hands on his bowed head, and prayed.

Thus the Spirit of Jesus led His servant to call new laborers into the harvest field and endow them with special qualifications for their work.

Leaving Lystra, Paul and his companions visited the

churches in the highland region of Phrygia and Galatia, everywhere distributing the letter of James. They next essayed to go into the populous and influential cities of Asia Minor, such as Colossae, Laodicaea, and Ephesus. What could they do better than bear the light of the Gospel to those teeming multitudes who sat in darkness and the shadow of death? Yet it was not to be: "They were forbidden of the Holy Spirit to speak the Word in Asia" (Acts 16:6).

The travellers therefore took a northern route, with the intention of entering the important province of Bithynia, lying along the shores of the Black Sea; but when they came to a point in the great Roman road, opposite Mysia, and were attempting to go out of Asia Minor into Bithynia, the spirit of Jesus suffered them not.

Checked when they attempted to go to the West, they were now stopped as they sought to go to the Northeast; and there was nothing for it but to keep straight on, until they came out at the terminus of the road, on the sea-coast, at the famous harbor of Troas, the ancient Troy. There they met with Luke whose presence is thenceforth denoted by the significant personal pronoun *we;* and thence the man of Macedonia beckoned the little missionary band across the straits to set up the banner of Christ on the hitherto untouched continent of Europe.

What an extremely attractive title that is for the Holy Spirit! He is preeminently the Spirit of Jesus. When Jesus was glorified, He was given in Pentecostal fulness, and the chief aim of His mission and ministry is to glorify the Lord Jesus and gather together the members of His Body, fitting them for union with their Head. He is also the Comforter and Guide of the saints until the church is presented faultless to her Lord; as Eliezer conducted Rebekah to his master's son.

It is interesting to study the method of His guidance as it was extended towards these early heralds of the Cross. It consisted largely in prohibitions, when they attempted to take another course than the right. When they would turn to the left, to Asia, He stayed them; and when they sought to turn to the right, to Bithynia, again He stayed them. He shut all the doors along their route, and bolted them; so that they had no alternative but to go straight forward. In the absence of any prohibition, they were left to gather that they were treading the prepared path for which they had been created in Christ Jesus.

Whenever you are doubtful as to your course, submit your judgment absolutely to the Spirit of God, and ask Him to shut against you every door but the right one. Say, "Blessed Spirit, I cast on Thee the entire responsibility of closing against my steps any and every course which is not of God. Let me hear Thy voice behind me whenever I turn to the right hand or the left. Put Thine arrest on me. Do not allow me."

In the meanwhile, continue along the path which you have been already treading. It lies in front of you; pursue it. Abide in the calling in which you were called. Keep on as you are, unless you are clearly told to do something else. Expect to have as clear a door out as you had in; and if there is no indication to the contrary, consider the absence of indication to be the indication of God's will that you are on His track.

The Spirit of Jesus waits to be to you, O pilgrim, what He was to Paul. Only be careful to obey His least prohibitions, and where, after believing prayer, there are no apparent hindrances, believe that you are on the way everlasting, and go forward with enlarged heart.

9
Ye Philippians

Acts 16

For a busy, footsore, heart-weary man, misunderstood and misrepresented, pursued by many anxieties and cares, there must be some place where the heated machinery can cool, and the soul unbend in the atmosphere of love and on the couch of tender sympathy. Even Jesus needed a Bethany. It is well when this is found within the precincts of home; when the door which shuts out the rush and glare of life shuts us in to love and sympathy, and those tender ministries which are the peculiar province of a woman's life. How little does the great world realize the large share that woman's influence has had in nourishing the patience and courage of its noblest heroes! In the privacy of the domestic life will be found those tender hands that wash the stripes, pour in the oil, and enable the soldier again to take the field.

To many, however, of the world's greatest benefactors, though they have stood in profound need of this tender sympathy, the home life has been denied. Theirs has been a solitary and lonely lot; partly because of the exigencies of their position, and partly because it has been difficult to find, or reveal themselves to, a kindred soul. This was largely the case with Paul. A self-contained, strong, heroic soul, he resembles the lofty mountains of his native Tarsus, whose slopes are clad with rich verdure and vegetation, while their summits rear themselves in steep and solitary majesty. Few have been dowered with a tenderer, warmer disposition.

The minute and particular greetings with which his Epistles close, the rain of hot tears in parting from his friends, his anguish of mind in having hurt those whom he was compelled to admonish and rebuke, his longing for companionship—are evidences of the genuineness and tenacity of his affection. But it was his appointed lot to have no settled dwelling place—no spot he could call home.

Yet the Apostle had marvelous powers of attracting men and women to himself. We have seen how he threw the mantle of his magnetic influence over Silas and Timothy; and the Galatians were ready to give him their eyes. But he was now to win a group of friends who would never cease to love him while life lasted; whoever else was alienated and weary, they would be true; whatever trouble threatened to engulf him, it would only elicit their more profuse ministrations; and Philippi was to become to him the one bright sunny spot in all the earth, more than Tarsus which had disowned him, more than Jerusalem which would cast him out, and next to the "far better" of Paradise.

Luke

The beloved physician seems to have met him first at Troas. Paul's temporary sojourn in the crowded ghetto may have induced a return of the acute disease from which he had suffered in Galatia, or he may have been laid low by malarial fever, to deal with which the nearest available physician was summoned, and this was Luke. In any case, here the two men met; and here in all likelihood the servant of God won his medical attendant for the Savior. In the enthusiasm of an ardent attachment the new disciple elected to become his fellow traveler, so as to be able at all times to minister to the much-suffering and frail tenement of his friend's dauntless and vehement spirit.

Lydia

She was probably a widow; a woman of considerable business capacity, with energy enough to leave her native city of

Thyatira, and cross the sea to establish herself in Philippi as agent for the sale of the purple-dyed garments for which her native town was famous. The word indicates that she disposed of the finest class of wares; and she must have possessed a considerable amount of capital to be able to deal in such expensive articles. She was withal an eager seeker after God.

On one memorable Sabbath, when only women were present, four strangers, Jews, appeared in the little circle, "sat down, and spake unto the women that were come together." This was the first Gospel sermon in Europe. And it is somewhat remarkable that it was addressed to a handful of women in the open air. Lydia was the first of a great succession of holy women, who have welcomed the Lord Jesus as their Sovereign and Spouse. And the open air has been the scene of the greatest victories of the Cross.

The result of that morning service was Lydia's conversion; whether she received the Apostle's message of the crucified and living Lord at once or gradually, is not clear—most likely her heart opened as a flower to the sun; but the result was that she, with her entire household, came over to believe in Jesus, whom Paul preached, and she felt as sure about her own conversion as she was eager for Paul to come and abide in her house: "If ye have judged me to be faithful unto the Lord, come into my house and abide there" (v. 15).

She must have been a woman of considerable determination and perseverance, to have overcome Paul's reluctance to be dependent on any of his converts. He would bear anything rather than risk the imputation of the suspicion that he was making profit out of the Gospel. Rather than this he wrought day and night, that he might be chargeable to none; and with his own hands ministered unto his own necessities and to those that were with him. But Lydia was able to override all his objections—"She constrained us," is Luke's reflection as he reviews the scene. So the four companions in travel found asylum and entertainment in her hospitable home.

We are inclined, therefore, to think of Lydia as a noble, truehearted, and devoted friend of the Apostle, who counted it her privilege as well as her joy that he should reap temporal benefits in return for the spiritual blessings which he had so richly sown in her heart; and her reward will be one day to hear from the Master's lips that in making the burdens of His servant lighter she had been ministering to Himself.

The Jailer

A rough, coarse man, probably! What else could be expected from one who had spent his early days in the Roman army, and his later ones amid the hardening and brutalizing experiences of a provincial Roman prison? The inner prison was a dark underground hole beneath his house (Acts 16:34); into this he thrust them; they would probably lie extended on the bare damp ground, their bleeding backs in contact with the soil, and their legs stretched to such an extent by the stocks as to almost dislocate their hips.

By midnight the two prisoners became so happy that they could no longer contain themselves, and began to sing, chanting the grand old Hebrew Psalms, and in the intervals praying. No doubt they were in the best of company, and found their souls overflowing with exuberant joy. "Bless the Lord, O my soul; and all that is within me, bless His holy name." It was an unwonted sound to the prisoners who stood or lay around in the pitch dark, their chains stapled to the walls—not one of them thought of sleep; "the prisoners," we are told, "were listening" (v. 25).

An earthquake broke in on the singing, the doors flew open, and the staples left their places. The jailer being roused from sleep came into the prison yard, and found the doors open. As Paul and Silas caught sight of him standing against glimmering starlight, to their horror they saw him draw his sword and prepare to kill himself rather than face an ignominious death for his infidelity to his charge. With a loud voice Paul arrested and reassured him; then the call for the light, the springing into the cell, the trembling limbs, the courtesy that led them out, the inquiry for salvation, the answer of peace, the motley midnight audience which gathered around the two servants of God, the loving tendance of their wounds, the baptism, the hastily prepared food, the glad rejoicing of the transformed believer and of all his believing house. One event crowding on the heels of another, and making a swift glad series of golden links which bound the jailer ever after to his Savior and to Paul.

He doubtless became one of the members of the Philippian church, a community of singular purity and loveliness, to whom the Apostle wrote his tenderest words without a syllable of rebuke. He could only thank God upon every remembrance of them, and in every supplication for them made request with joy. They were beloved and longed for, his joy and crown. He longed after them all in the tender mercies of Christ Jesus. They were his Bethany, his Zarephath, his Well of Bethlehem.

10

In Weakness and Fear

Acts 18

Five hours' sail across the Saronic Bay brought the Apostle to
Cenchrea, the port of Corinth to the east; for this great and
busy city commanded two waterways. This commanding position thus gave her a quite unusual importance in the eye of
the Apostle, ever eager to seize on any advantage which he
could use for the Gospel of his Lord. To establish a strong
Christian church there would be to cast seeds of Christian
teaching on waters that would bear them east and west.
Christian missionaries should be strategists, expending their
strength where populations teem and rivers of world-wide
influence have their rise.

But the Apostle entered the proud and beautiful city "in
weakness, and fear, and much trembling." He could not
forget the frigid contempt which he had encountered at
Athens, and which was harder to bear than violent opposition. He may have been suffering from some aggravation of
his habitual trouble, without Luke's presence to treat it; and
he was profoundly conscious of being deficient in those gifts
of learning and eloquence on which the Corinthians set such
store. He knew that his speech and his preaching could never
be in persuasive words of human wisdom, and it was his
fixed determination to know nothing among them but Jesus
Christ, and Him crucified.

There were many other difficulties to be encountered,
which made his ministry in Corinth the more difficult, and

his consequent success the more conspicuous.

The Value of Continual Work

In his first Epistle to Corinth, he lays great emphasis on this. Always maintaining the right of those who preached the Gospel to live by the Gospel, he did not use it; but suffered all things rather than hinder its progress or influence. No chance should be given to the merchants and traders that thronged the city from all parts, prepared to sacrifice everything for purposes of gain, to allege that he was actuated by mercenary motives. He, therefore, resumed his trade of tent-making, and was thankful to come across two Christian Jews who had been flung on this shore by the decree of the Emperor, which expelled all Jews from Rome. With them, therefore, he abode and wrought, for they were of the same craft; and a friendship sprang up between him and Aquila, with his wife Priscilla, which was destined to have an important bearing on the spread of Christianity in the metropolis from which they had come, and in Ephesus, to which they would accompany their newly made friend. Perhaps Paul was in their employ; but in any case work was short and wages scant, so that he was not unfrequently in actual want (2 Cor. 11:9; 1 Cor. 4:11, 12).

The Virulent Hatred of the Jews

According to his usual practice, Paul betook himself every Sabbath to the synagogue, and reasoned, persuading the Jews and Greek proselytes that the conception of the Hebrew Scriptures was precisely that of a suffering and crucified Messiah. This went on for some weeks; but the measure of his labors was somewhat curtailed by the heavy drain of his daily toil. It was not till Timothy and Silas arrived, the one from Thessalonica, and the other from Berea, bringing cheering news of the steadfastness of his converts, their hands full of generous benefactions, that he was able to give himself with more leisure and intensity to the cherished object of his life. "He was pressed in the spirit, and testified to the Jews that Jesus was Christ" (v. 5).

This was more than the influential men of the Jewish community could bear; they opposed, blasphemed, and drove him from the synagogue.

Their hatred culminated when the Apostle gladly accepted the offer of a God-fearing proselyte, Titus Justus, whose house was close to the synagogue, to hold meetings there. Among those that migrated with the Apostle from the synagogue was Crispus, its chief ruler, who believed in the Lord with all his house. Many of the people of Corinth, also, heard, believed, and were baptized. As the new meeting-house became more crowded, and the movement increased in numbers and influence, the Jews became more and more exasperated, and at last rose in a body, seized Paul, and dragged him before the Roman Governor, who happened to be Gallio, brother to Seneca, the famous philosopher, and Nero's tutor. He was a man of unusual culture and refinement, sweetness, and lovableness. He represented the broad and liberal views of educated Romans, of the policy that Rome should exercise towards the various religions of the provinces; and when he discovered that the charge against Paul was of no imperial importance, and had to do indeed not with facts, or civil wrong or moral outrage, but with words, and names, and Jewish law, he would have nothing more to do with it or them, but bade his lictors drive them from the judgment seat.

Paul's Converts

Corinth has been compared to Paris for its vice; to New-market for the preponderance of the sporting interest; to Chicago for the mixture of its population; to Vanity Fair for its frivolity and lightness. Thither gathered the scum of the world. Soldiers and sailors, slaves and prostitutes, jockeys and chariot drivers, athletes and wrestlers; Romans with their imperial bearing; Greeks with their regular features;

Jews with their unmistakable badge; Scythians from the shores of the Black Sea; men of Mesopotamia, Pontus, Egypt, and Asia Minor—all bent on business or amusement, and daubed to a greater or less extent with the exceeding evil of this grossly impure city.

To such a city Paul opened his message, encouraged by the assurance of the Lord that He had much people there. How often to His tried and persecuted servants does the Master come as He came to the Apostle! They may be conscious of weakness and much fear, may speak His word in trembling, may be derided as a spectacle and laughingstock, may be encompassed with toil and pain and persecution; but He stands beside in a vision, and says: "Be not afraid, but speak, and hold not thy peace: for I am with thee, and no man shall set on thee to hurt thee."

With this encouragement in his heart, Paul labored for a year and six months in this gay and sinful city, with marvelous success. It is true that not many of the wise, or mighty, or noble of this world, were among the chosen ones; they who were accounted as weak, and base, and contemptible, by the highbred leaders of Corinthian society were selected as the foundation stones of the newly gathered church. There might be a Crispus and Gaius, a Stephanas and his household, all of whom, contrary to his usual practice, the Apostle baptized before Timothy and Silas arrived; but these were exceptions to the general rule. Perhaps women preponderated in the young community, as the Apostle devotes so much space in his Epistle to regulating their behavior. We know, at least, of Phoebe, the deaconess of the church at Cenchrea, who bore his epistle to Rome; and of Chloe, whose household slaves were the medium of intelligence when Paul was at Ephesus.

The majority of his converts, however, were of the lowest caste, and of those who had been deeply stained with the vices that made Corinth notorious. The city was the resort of fornicators, idolaters, adulterers, effeminates, thieves, covetous, drunkards, revilers, and extortioners, and such had they been; but under the preaching of the Cross, in the power of the Holy Ghost, a marvelous change had passed over them—they had become washed, sanctified, and justified, in the name of the Lord Jesus, and in the Spirit of our God. Jesus had become their wisdom, righteousness, sanctification, and redemption.

What a contrast between that little Church and the great heathen world out of which it had been chosen! We may imagine one of its meetings toward the close of the Apostle's visit. It is a Sabbath evening. Outside, the streets are full of pleasure seekers and revellers. Groups of idlers are discussing the last chariot race, or staking their money on an approaching boxing match. But within the little meeting place all is hushed and still. Paul is speaking of things which eye hath not seen, nor ear heard, nor the heart of man conceived; or the men in turn are contributing to the edification of the rest, with a psalm, or a teaching, or a revelation, or the interpretation of an unknown tongue; while the women, modestly veiled, listen in silence. Now the Love feast is being partaken of, each bringing some contribution of victuals to the common store; and presently the Lord's Supper will conclude the evening engagements, partaken of according to the method delivered to the Apostle by the Lord Jesus Himself (I Cor. 11 and 12).

This was a marvelous sequel to his timid and unadorned entrance among them. But it is evident that the Apostle was far from satisfied. He complained that he could not speak unto them as unto spiritual; but as unto carnal, as unto babes in Christ; that he was obliged to feed them with milk, and not with meat. He, doubtless, detected the first working of that unhallowed leaven which was afterwards to break out in such fearful ferment. It must have been, therefore, with no small misgiving that he tore himself away at the close of his protracted sojourn, leaving the infant community to the tendance of God with much of the same solicitude with which Jochebed launched the cradle ark on the tawny waters of the Nile.

But though he left the city, it produced an ineffaceable effect upon his methods of thought and expression. Years afterwards we find him alluding to the mingling of gold, silver, and precious stones, with wood, hay, and stubble, in the construction of temples and other buildings; or comparing the body to a temple; or drawing illustrations from the boxing match and the arena, the triumphal procession and the threatrical representation. It seemed as though his speech were dyed with the coloring borrowed from the spectacles with which he had grown so familiar in the streets of Corinth.

At last, however, he resolved to leave Corinth. Many reasons prompted this step, and among them the desire to proceed to Jerusalem to ascertain the feeling of the mother church. And thus the first memorable missionary tour in Greece came to an end, and for the fourth time since his conversion the Apostle approached the city which was doubly dear to him—memories of his Lord being now entwined with the sacred associations of David, Solomon, Hezekiah, and Ezra.

11
More Than a Conqueror

Acts 19

It was toward the close of Paul's third missionary journey. About three years before, he had left the Syrian Antioch for the third time, after a sojourn of some duration (Acts 18:23). His eager spirit could not rest amid the comparative comfort and ease of the vigorous church life which was establishing itself there, but yearned with tender solicitude over his converts throughout the region of Galatia and Phrygia. He therefore again passed the Cilician Gates, traversed the bleak tablelands of the upper or highland country, stablishing all the disciples, and working towards the Roman province of Asia. This lay to the southwest, on the seaboard. He had been previously forbidden to enter it (Acts 16:6); but his steps were now as clearly led to it as they had formerly been restrained. Thus does our Sovereign Lord withhold His servants from the immediate fulfilment of their dreams, that they may return to them again when the time is ripe, and they, too, are more thoroughly equipped. The experiences of Paul in Greece were of the utmost possible service in fitting him for his ministry in this thickly populated and highly civilized district; which resulted in a work of evangelization throughout the neighborhood, and in the ultimate formation of those seven churches, to which the risen Lord addressed His final messages.

It was to redeem a pledge he had solemnly made that the Apostle at last came down to Ephesus. He had spent one

Sabbath day there previously, on his way from Corinth to Jerusalem. On that occasion his ministrations had so deeply interested the Jews, that they had urged him to abide for a longer period; but this being impossible, on account of the necessity of hastening to Jerusalem to fulfil his vow, when taking his leave of them he said, "I will return again unto you, if the Lord will" (Acts 18:21). It was in fulfilment of that promise that the Apostle now visited the metropolis of Asia the Less.

He probably but dimly realized as he entered Ephesus how long he would remain, or the far-reaching results of his residence. It was enough for him to realize, as he afterwards wrote to the Ephesian converts, that there was a prepared path awaiting him; but whether it should be smooth or rough was known only to Him whose he was and whom he served.

The Battlefield
In the first place there was the pressure of the strange, eager mass of human beings, whose interests, aims, and methods of thought were so foreign to his own. No one has stood alone in the midst of Benares, surrounded by that vast heathen population, worshipping on the banks of the brown and muddy Ganges, or ascending the thousand stairs of the marble temples which extend along the riverside, without a sense of loneliness and isolation. How can he hope to affect India's habits of thought and life—he might as well attempt to divert the course of the ancient stream. Did not Paul feel thus, as he spent his first week at Ephesus?

But, besides, there was the vast system of organized idolatry which centered in the temple of Diana. Her image was said to have fallen from Jupiter (possibly a meteorite), and it was enshrined in a temple, counted to be one of the wonders of the world. The magnificence of uncalculated wealth, the masterpieces of human art, the fame of splendid ceremonials, the lavish gifts of emperors and kings, the attendance and service of thousands of priests and priestesses, combined to give it an unrivalled eminence of influence and prestige. Sooner might some humble Protestant missionary working in a back street of Rome expect to dim the magnificence of St. Peter's, or diminish the attendance of its vast congregations, as Paul hope that his residence in Ephesus could have any effect whatever on the worship of Diana.

In connection with the temple there throve a great trade in amulets and charms. Each individual in the vast crowds that came up to worship at the shrine was eager to carry back some memento of his visit, and the more so if the keepsake would serve as a preservative against evil omens and spirits, of which there was a great and constant dread. The trade in these articles must have been a large one, or the artificers in silver would not have been numerous enough to fill the city with confusion, and to necessitate the interference of the town clerk. What the trade in strong drink is among ourselves, that was the business in these miniature shrines manufactured by Demetrius and his fellow craftsmen. How impossible it seemed that one man, in three years, employing only moral and spiritual weapons, could make any difference to this ancient and extensive craft!

But still further, like many of the cities of the time, filled with motley populations—part Oriental and part Greek— Ephesus was deeply infected with the black arts of the exorcist, the magician, and the professor of cabalistic mysteries. It is no child's play to turn a nation of savages from their confidence in witchcraft and medicine men to sane views of life and Divine Providence; but how much harder to neutralize such insidious poison as wrought through a great city like Ephesus! The people fixed the days of marriage and journeying, the engagements they should make, and the business transactions on which they should enter, after an appeal to the soothsayers and magicians; and it was a formidable task to combat their rooted prejudices and habits.

But perhaps Paul's most inveterate foe was the Jewish synagogue, entrenched in ancient prejudices and persistent disbelief. They were hardened and disobedient, speaking

evil of "the Way" before the multitude. He also recalls, in his
farewell address to the Ephesian elders, the trials which befell him by the plots of the Jews. When the great riot broke
out, they were only too glad to show their hatred of the
Christians by putting forward Alexander to disavow all connection with them.

Such were the giant obstacles that confronted the humble
tentmaker, as he settled down to his trade in company with
Aquila and Priscilla. But he looked far beyond the limits of
his workshop to great victories for his Lord, much as Carey,
who wrought at his cobbling with a map of the world in front
of him. But greater was He that was for him than all that
there were against him, and in all these things he was destined to be more than a conqueror, through Him that had
loved him.

The Evidence

Let us turn to the Acts of the Apostles, and ask if Paul were
indeed more than conqueror. The answer is unmistakable.
After three months' conflict with the Jews in their
synagogue, the Apostle was driven to the course he was
wont to adopt under similar circumstances—he moved his
disciples to the schoolhouse of one Tyrannus, and taught
there daily, as soon as noon was past, and a pause put alike
on the labors of the schoolmaster and the artisan. In consequence of these ministrations, "all they which dwelt in Asia
heard the word of the Lord Jesus, both Jews and Greeks"
(v.10)—a very strong statement, when we bear in mind the
populousness of that crowded province. Even the sil-
versmiths who caused the riot acknowledged that not only at
Ephesus, but almost throughout all Asia, Paul had persuaded
and turned away much people; and there was great danger
that the temple would be depleted of its worshippers, and
Diana deposed from her magnificence.

With respect to the trade in amulets and charms, it fell off
so seriously that the craftsmen realized that unless they be-
stirred themselves their gains would be at an end.

With respect to the strongly entrenched position of the magicians and exorcists, they were utterly baffled and confounded by the much greater miracles which were wrought through Paul; so much so that the handkerchiefs he used to wipe the sweat from his brow and the aprons in which he wrought at his trade, were made the medium of healing virtue as they were carried from his person to the sick and demon possessed. So mighty was the impression that Christ had secrets superior to the best contained in their ancient books, that many of them that had believed came confessing, and declaring their deeds. And not a few of those who practiced magical arts brought their books together in one of the open squares and burned them in the sight of all. So mightily grew the word of the Lord, and prevailed.

With respect to the exorcist Jews, they, too, were silenced. It would appear that the name of Jesus, spoken even by those that did not believe in Him, had a potency over evil spirits such as no other name exerted; and it had been blasphemously used by strolling Jews, who had taken upon themselves to call that sweet and holy Name over some that were possessed. But in one notable instance the demon himself had remonstrated, crying, "Jesus I know, and Paul I know; but who are ye?" (v. 15) and he had leaped on them, and mastered them, so that they fled from the house naked and wounded.

The Source of Victory
If we turn from his outward life to study the diary of this wonderful man, who seemed single-handed in his conflicts and victories, we find a pathetic record of his sorrows and trials. Writing during these eventful months, he speaks of himself as a man doomed to death and made a spectacle to the world; for Christ's sake, a fool, weak, and dishonored; suffering hunger and thirst, when work was scant and ill-paid; having no certain dwelling place, because unable to hold a situation long together through the plotting of his foes; hated, buffeted, reviled, persecuted, defamed; made as

the filth of the world, and the offscouring of all things (1 Cor. 4:9-13).

When he tells the story of the affliction which befell him during his residence in Asia, he says that he was weighed down exceedingly beyond his power, insomuch that he despaired even of life; that he was pressed on every side, perplexed, pursued, smitten down, groaning in the tabernacle of his body, and always bearing about the dying of the Lord Jesus. In addition to all these things that were without, there pressed on him daily the care of all the churches. There was also his anxiety about individuals, as he ceased not to admonish every one of them night and day with tears (2 Cor. 1:8; 4:8; 9:27, 28).

As the result of it all we wonder how such a man, under such drawbacks and in face of such opposing forces, could be more than a conqueror. Evidently we are driven to seek the source of his victory outside himself. It was through Him that loved. He not only overcame, but he was more than an overcomer; he overcame with ease; he brought off the spoils of victory—and this because he was in daily communication with One who had loved, did love, and would love him, world without end; and who was ever pouring reinforcements into his soul, as men will pour fresh oxygen air to their comrade who is groping for pearls in the depth of the sea.

The only matter about which the Apostle, therefore, felt any anxiety was whether anything could occur to cut him off from the living, loving Lord. "Can anything separate me from the love of Christ?"—that was the only question worth consideration.

We strangely misjudge the love of God. We think that our distresses and sufferings, our sins and failures, may make Him love us less, whereas they will draw Him nearer, and make His love exert itself more evidently and tenderly.

Oh, blessed love that comes down to us from the heart of Jesus, the essence of the eternal love of God dwelling there and coming through Jesus to us—nothing can ever staunch, nothing exhaust, nothing intercept it! It will not let us go. It

leaps the gulf of space unattenuated, it bridges time un-
exhausted. It does not depend on our reciprocation or response. It is not our love that holds God, but God's that holds
us. Not our love to Him, but His to us. And since nothing
can separate us from the love of God, He will go on loving us
for ever, and pouring into us the entire fulness of His life and
glory; so that whatever our difficulties, whatever our weakness and infirmity, whatever the barrels of water which
drench the sacrifice and the wood on which it lies, we shall
be kept steadfast, unmovable, always abounding in the work
of the Lord, gaining by our losses, succeeding by our failures, triumphing in our defeats, and ever more conquerors
through Him that loved us.

12

The Furtherance of the Gospel

Acts 19

That was the one thing Paul cared for. If only the Gospel of
the love of God made progress, and the Lord Jesus were
magnified, he was more than content to suffer to the uttermost. And now, as he reviews the things which had happened to him from the standpoint of the years, he rejoices
with exceeding joy to be able to announce to his brethren at
Philippi that they had fallen out to the furtherance of the
Gospel.

Our space forbids us to tell in detail the story of his trans-
portation from the lower platform of the Temple at Jerusalem
to the hired house at Rome; but we may at least consider its
successive stages beneath the light of the thought, which
gave him such pleasure, that they had all conducted to the
furtherance of the Gospel, partly by giving him an opportunity of manifesting the traits of a true Christian character,
and partly by enabling him to give his testimony for Jesus
before the highest tribunals in the world.

First, there was the awful riot in the Temple court. The Jews
of Asia, perhaps led by Alexander the coppersmith, laid hold
of Paul, under the impression that he had introduced
Trophimus, whom they knew as an Ephesian, into the court
reserved for Jews. They dragged him down the steps, furi-
ously beating him the while, and with the intent of murder-
ing him when they reached the bottom. With the greatest
difficulty he was rescued by Lysias and his legionaires, who

rushed down from the adjoining Castle of Antonia, surrounded him with their shields, and bore him back on their
shoulders from the frenzied vehemence of the mob. It was
not simply the result of natural coolness and self-command,
but because he was at rest in Christ, and desired to magnify
his Master, that he was able to hold a brief conversation with
his deliverer in the midst of the tumult, and obtain permis-
sion to address the people in their national tongue, weaving
the story of the risen Jesus so ingeniously into his personal
narrative, that they could do no other than listen.

There was a manly strength in his quiet remonstrance with
those who were set to examine him by scourging, and avowal of Roman citizenship, which must have filled them
with profound respect. Here was no common criminal!

That his efforts to use these trying scenes for the glory of
his Master were appreciated and accepted was made abun-
dantly clear by the vision of the Lord, who bade him be of
good cheer, and assured him that the witness which he had
given from the steps of the castle and in the halls of the
Sanhedrin should be repeated in Rome herself, at the very
heart of the empire, where all the Gentiles should hear.

There must have been something very noble and heroic in
his bearing; or his nephew, who was evidently in the secrets
of his foes, and must have passed as a bigoted Jew, would
never have run the risk of being torn limb from limb for
divulging the secret plot of the zealots, who had bound
themselves by a solemn vow neither to eat nor drink till they
had for ever silenced the tongue that gave them more cause
to fear than all the legions of Felix's escort.

His Judicial Trials. He was presently hurried by a strong
body of soldiers in a forced march, by night, to Antipatris,
thirty-five miles distant, and twenty-five miles further, on
the following day, to Caesarea, to undergo trial before Felix,
the Roman Governor of Judea. But as on repeated occasions
he stood before him, he seemed less eager for himself, and
bent on snatching every opportunity of so public a position
to explain the nature of "the Way," and to reason with his

judge concerning the faith in Christ Jesus. Indeed, on one occasion he spoke so powerfully of righteousness, self-control, and judgment to come, in the presence of Felix and the woman with whom he was living in adultery, that Felix trembled as the prisoner compelled him to review a life of shameless infamy beneath the searchlight of an awakened conscience.

When Festus came in the room of Felix, who had been recalled in disgrace, the Apostle, within a few days, so far impressed the newcomer with his faith in Jesus, who had died, but whom he affirmed to be alive, that the Governor was able to state the case with wonderful accuracy to King Agrippa, who, with his sister Bernice, came to pay their respects to the new representative of the Emperor.

But perhaps Paul's greatest opportunity, and one of which he availed himself to the full, was that in which he was able to preach the Gospel to an assembly that comprised all the fashion, wealth, and distinction of the land. Festus was there in state, and the Herods, brother and sister, seated on golden chairs; the officers of the garrison, and the principal men of the city. How great a contrast between the splendid pomp of that occasion and the poor chained prisoner at the bar! Yet, in truth, though bending under the weight of sixty years and many sorrows, he was the noblest and fairest decked of all the glittering throng. How grandly he preached Christ that day under the guise of making his defense! The story of the suffering and risen Lord; the fulfilment of the predictions of Moses and the prophets; the opening of eyes; the turning from darkness to light; the conditions of remitted sin and an inheritance among the saints—such topics were recited with all the passionate earnestness of which he was capable, till the Roman thought him mad, and the Jew princeling needed all his courtly wit to turn aside the barbed dart of the prisoner's appeal.

Caesarea. In one of the guardrooms of the old palace of the Caesars, for two whole years, Paul was kept a prisoner, but permitted to see, and receive help from, his friends. How gladly must the saints in Caesarea and from other places have availed themselves of the privilege! It is an old tradition that during this period Luke wrote the Third Gospel, in fellowship with his friend, and under his direction. If this were so, what an unfailing source of interest it must have been to the two to trace the course of all things accurately from the first, as they delivered them, which from the beginning were eye-witnesses and ministers of the Word. In another way that period of two years was very fruitful in the best sense. Paul's appreciation of the truth as it is in Jesus, was greatly ripened and deepened. Contrast the Epistles to the *Thessalonians, Corinthians, Romans,* and *Galatians,* with those to the *Ephesians, Philippians,* and *Colossians,* and the advance is easily discernible. Less polemics and defense of his motives and actions, and more of the believer's vital union with his Lord; less doctrinal discussion of the work of Christ, and more absorption in His Person; less of the old covenant, more of the new, of the King, and of the life in the heavenlies. Ah! those years spent within view of the dividing sea, restrained by the old castle walls, and the chain which he shook so pathetically before Festus and his guests, notwithstanding that the indomitable spirit was stayed from its incessant labors and journeys, were turned to good account, if only they enabled him to give the church his priceless prison Epistles.

At last this term of confinement came to an end. The ecclesiastical authorities had never ceased to urge that he should be handed over to their jurisdiction, a claim which in God's good providence the Roman Governors steadfastly refused. They knew, and Paul knew, that to such a trial there would be only one end. But finally, when Festus showed signs of yielding, Paul claimed his right as a Roman citizen to have his case tried by the Emperor himself, partly because it would remove it from local prejudice, partly because he desired to secure for the Christian church the same recognition as was awarded to the Jewish synagogue, and partly that he might fulfil his long-cherished purpose of proclaiming the Gospel in Rome.

To that appeal nothing to the contrary could be alleged. He had appealed to Caesar, and to Caesar he must go.

The Voyage

At every stage of it the Apostle seems to have bent all his endeavors to use his opportunities, as far as possible, for the glory of his Lord. To him to live was Christ. He reckoned always and everywhere that he was a debtor to all men, and under obligation to repay to each some proportion of the momentous debt he owed for his redemption.

They set sail, first in an ordinary sailing vessel, then from Myra, in an Alexandrian grain ship, one of the great fleet perpetually engaged in provisioning Rome. Contrary to Paul's advice, who even at this stage of the voyage must have been considered as a person of distinction and experience, the captain attempted to cross the open bay from the Fair Havens to Phoenice, and each on the southern side of Crete. But, when halfway across, the wind changed, and a sudden squall struck down from the mountains and carried the big ship out to sea. Three days after, all hands (even of the prisoners) were called in to lighten the ship, by casting out cargo and other movables; and after many days of storm, in which neither sun nor moon appeared, all hope that they should be saved gradually faded away.

It was then that Paul stood forth, calm, assured, with the message of God, to cheer and reanimate their fainting hearts. Like Peter before his execution, the servant of God had quietly slept amid the tumult. Like Peter, too, he had been ministered to by angels. Through the murky atmosphere one of these ministering spirits had found his way to his side, uttering a "Fear not!" fresh from the throne, and an assurance that he should yet stand before Caesar. Evidently the deliverance of the crew had been previously the subject of the Apostle's prayer; for the angel added, "Lo! there have been granted unto thee by God all they that sail with thee." Here was an opportunity of preaching faith in God, and belief in the power of prayer.

Always full of prompt common-sense, he detected the attempt of the sailors, when the vessel struck, to get away in the boat; but with something above common-sense, with a sense of the Eternal and Divine, he took bread, and as though he were presiding at the Lord's table in Corinth or Philippi, he gave thanks to God in the presence of all, and broke it, and began to eat.

When they reached the shore of Malta on that drear November morning, it seemed as though nothing more could be done to further the Gospel. But as the viper fell off Paul's hand, and the father of the chief man in the island was healed of dysentery through his prayer, and all else who had diseases throughout the island were cured by his touch, much was done to magnify Him, concerning whom Paul was proud to say, "Whose I am, and whom I serve."

Rome

Did his heart misgive him as he at last approached the city, and signs of her splendor and teeming life multiplied at every step? He had often thought of this moment, and longed for it. Some three years before, writing to the church at Rome, he said, "I long to see you, that I may impart some spiritual gift" (Rom. 1:11). He confessed that he had often prayed and purposed to come to them. But he had never anticipated coming like this—one of a knot of prisoners in charge of Roman legionaires. But almost certainly through his bonds he was able to effect very much more good than if he had been free. Had he been free, he might have gone from synagogue to synagogue, but the opportunity would never have befallen him of speaking to the Pretorian guard and Caesar's household.

It is thus that God answers our prayers in ways and methods we did not expect. We have set our hearts on realizing some project. For long years it has gleamed before us as an Alp through its long-drawn valley. We have yearned, prayed, and wrought for it night and day. Assurances have been borne in upon our souls that one day we shall rejoice in a realization of our cherished desires. But when at last we come to our Rome, it is as prisoners, and our hands in fetters.

Do not fret at the limitations and disabilities of your life. They are required as the makeweight, and constitute your opportunity. Storm and shipwreck, centurion and sea-captain, soldier and fetter, Caesarea and Rome—all are part of the plan, all work together for good, all are achieving God's ideal, and making you what, in your best hours, you have asked to become.

13

In a Strait, Betwixt Two

Acts 28

Through the providence of God, and probably by the kind intervention of the centurion—who had conceived a sincere admiration for him during these months of travel together, and who, indeed, owed him his life—Paul, on his arrival in Rome, was treated with great leniency. He was permitted to hire a house or apartment in the near neighborhood of the great Pretorian barracks, and live by himself, the only sign of his captivity consisting in the chain that fastened his wrist to a Roman legionary, the soldiers relieving each other every four or six hours.

There were many advantages in this arrangement. It secured him from the hatred of his people, and gave him a marvelous opportunity of casting the seeds of the Gospel into the head of the rivers of population, that poured from the metropolis throughout the known world. At the same time, it must have been very irksome. Always to be in the presence of another, and that other filled with Gentile antipathy to Jewish habits and Pagan irresponsiveness to Christian fervor; to be able to make no movement without the clanking of his chain, and the consent of his custodian; to have to conduct his conferences, utter his prayers, and indite his epistles, beneath those stolid eyes, or amid brutal and blasphemous interruptions—all this must have been excessively trying to a sensitive temperament like the Apostle's. That must have been a hard and long schooling, which had taught him to be content even with this, for the sake of the Gospel. But this, also, he could do through Christ that strengthened him. And it also turned out greatly to the furtherance of the cause he loved. Many of these brawny veterans became humble, earnest disciples. With a glow of holy joy, he informs the Philippians, that his bonds in Christ have become manifest throughout the whole Pretorian guard; and we know that this was the beginning of a movement destined within three centuries to spread throughout the entire army, and compel Constantine to adopt Christianity as the religion of the State. This was a blessed issue of that period of suffering which so often extorted the cry, "Remember my bonds" (Col. 4:18).

It might be said of the Apostle, as of his Lord, that they came to him from every quarter. Timothy, his son in the faith; Mark, now "profitable"; Luke, with his quick physician's eye and delicate sympathy; Aristarchus, who shared his imprisonment, that he might have an opportunity of ministering to his needs; Tychicus, from Ephesus, "the beloved brother and faithful minister in the Lord"; Epaphras, from Colossae, a "beloved fellow servant, and faithful minister of Christ," on the behalf of the church there; Epaphroditus, from Philippi, who brought the liberal contributions of the beloved circle, that for so many years had never ceased to remember their friend and teacher; Demas, who had not yet allowed the present to turn him aside from the eternal and unseen—these, and others, are mentioned in the postscripts of his Epistles as being with him. Members of the Roman church would always be welcomed, and must have poured into his humble lodging in a perpetual stream; Epaenetus and Mary, Andronicus and Junia, Tryphena and Tryphosa, Persis the beloved, and Apelles the approved, must often have resorted to that apartment, which was irradiated with the perpetual presence of the Lord. They had come to meet him on his first arrival as far as the Appii Forum and the Three Taverns, and would not be likely to neglect him, now he was settled among them.

Then what interest would be aroused by the episodes of

those two years! The illness of Epaphroditus, who was sick unto death; the discovery and conversion of Onesimus, the runaway slave; the writing and dispatch of the Epistles, which bear such evident traces of the prison cell. There could have been no lack of incident, amid the interest of which the two years must have sped by more swiftly than the other two years spent in confinement at Caesarea.

It is almost certain that Paul was acquitted at his first trial, and liberated, and permitted for two or three years at least to engage again in his beloved work. He was evidently expecting this, when, writing to the Philippians, he said: "I myself am confident in the Lord, that I myself, too, shall come speedily." In his letter to Philemon also, he goes so far as to ask that a lodging may be prepared for him, as he hopes to be granted to their prayers. Universal tradition affirms an interspace of liberty between his two imprisonments; and without this hypothesis, it is almost impossible to explain many of the incidental allusions of the Epistles to Timothy and Titus, which cannot refer, so far as we can see, to the period that falls within the compass of the Acts.

Whether his liberation were due to the renewed offices of the centurion, or to more explicit reports received from Caesarea, history does not record; but it was by the decree of a greater than Nero that the coupling chain was struck off the Apostle's wrist, and he was free to go where he would. That he should abide in the flesh was, in the eye of the great Head of the Church, needful for the furtherance and joy of faith to the little communities that looked to him as their father; and their rejoicing was destined to be more abundant in Jesus Christ by his coming to them again.

Once more a free man, Paul would certainly fulfil his intention of visiting Philemon and the church of Colossae. Thence he would make his way to the church at Ephesus, to hold further converse with them on those sacred mysteries which in his Epistle he had commenced to unfold. It was probably during his residence that Onesiphorus ministered to him with such tender thoughtfulness as to elicit a significant reference in the last Epistle (2 Timothy 1:18). Leaving Timothy behind him with the injunction to command some that they should preach no other Gospel than they had heard from his lips (1 Timothy 1:3), he travelled onward to Macedonia and Philippi.

From Philippi he must have passed to other churches in Greece, and among the rest to Corinth. Finally he set sail with Titus for Crete, where he left him to set in order the things that were wanting, and to appoint elders in every city (Titus 1:5). On his return to the mainland he wrote an epistle to Titus, from the closing messages in which we gather that he was about to winter at Nicopolis surrounded by several friends, such as Artemas, Zenas, Tychicus, and Apollos, who were inspired with his own spirit, and were gladly assisting him in strengthening the organization and purifying the teaching in these young churches, each of which had possibly to pass through some such phases of doctrinal and practical difficulty as are reflected in the mirror of the Epistles to Corinth (1 Cor. 3:12, 13).

This blessed liberty, however, was summarily cut short. One of the most terrible events in the history of the ancient world—the burning of Rome—took place in the year A.D. 64; and to divert from himself the suspicion which indicated him as its author, Nero accused the Christians of being the incendiaries. Immediately the fierce flames of the first general persecution broke out. Those who were resident in the metropolis, and who must have been well knwon and dear to the Apostle, were seized and subjected to horrible barbarities, while a strict search was made throughout the empire for their leaders, the Jews abetting the inquisitors. It was not likely that so eminent a Christian as the Apostle would escape.

He was staying for a time at Troas, in the house of Carpus, where he had arrived from Nicopolis. His arrest was so sudden that he had not time to gather up his precious books and parchments, which may have included copies of his Epistles, a Hebrew Bible, and some early copies of the sayings of our

Lord; or to wrap around him the cloak which had been his companion in many a wintry storm. Thence he was hurried to Rome.

A little group of friends accompanied him, with faithful tenacity, in this last sad journey. Demas and Crescens, Titus and Tychicus, Luke and Erastus. But Erastus abode at Corinth, through which the little band may have passed; and Trophimus fell ill at Miletus, and had to be left there, as the Roman guard would brook no delay. So, for the second time, Paul reached Rome.

But the circumstances of his second imprisonment differed widely from those of the first. Then he had his own hired house; now he was left in close confinement, and tradition points to the Mamertine prison as the scene of his last weeks or months. Then he was easily accessible; now Onesiphorus had to seek him out very diligently, and it took some courage not to be ashamed of his chain. Then he was the center of a large circle of friends and sympathizers; now the winnowing fan of trouble had greatly thinned their ranks, while others had been dispatched on distant missions. "Only Luke is with me" (II Timothy 4:11), is the rather sad expression of the old man's loneliness. Then he cherished a bright hope of speedy liberation; now, though he had successfully met the first impeachment, which was probably one of incendiarism, and had been delivered out of the mouth of the lion, he had no hope of meeting the second, which would include the general charge of introducing new customs hostile to the stability of the imperial government. Its very vagueness made it so hard to combat, and it was inevitable that he should be caught within its meshes.

But it caused him no sorrow. In earlier days he had greatly set his heart on being clothed upon with the body that was from heaven, and on being suddenly caught up to be for ever with the Lord. It seemed unlikely now that such would be the method of his transition to that rest of which he had spoken so pathetically. Not by the triumphant path of the air, but by the darksome path of death and the grave, would he pass into the presence of the Lord. It was, however, a matter of small importance what would be the method of his home going; he was only too thankful, on his review of his career, to say humbly and truthfully, "I have striven the good strife, I have finished my course, I have kept the faith; hence-forth there is laid up for me a crown of righteousness" (II Timothy 4:8).

How characteristic it is to find him boasting of the great audience of Gentiles, to whom, at the first stage of his trial, he was able fully to proclaim the Gospel message. It is equally characteristic to hear him affirm that the ease and success of his witness bearing was due, not to himself, but to the conscious nearness of his Lord, who stood by and strengthened him.

What were the following processes of that trial? How long was he kept in suspense? Did Timothy arrive in time to see him, and to be with him at the last supreme moment? What was the exact method of his martyrdom? To these questions there is no certain reply. Tradition points to a spot, about three miles from Rome, on the Ostian road, where, at the stroke of the headsman's axe, he was beheaded, and his spirit leaving its frail tenement, entered the house not made with hands, eternal in the heavens.

But how vast the contrast between that scene, which may have excited but little interest, save to the friends that mingled in the little group, and that other scene, in which an abundant entrance was ministered to this noble spirit, as it entered the presence of the Lord! If Christ arose to receive Stephen, may He not also have stood up to welcome Paul? Again he beheld the face that had looked down on him from the opened heavens at his conversion, and heard the voice that had called him by his name. His long-cherished wish of being "with Christ" was gratified, and he found it "far better" than he had ever thought.

His was now the inheritance of the saints in light, of which the Holy Spirit had been the earnest and first fruits. He had passed the goal, and had attained to the prize of his high calling in Christ. He had been found in Christ, not having his own righteousness, but the righteousness which is of God by faith. No castaway was he! As he had kept Christ's deposit, so Christ had kept his. And as he gave in the account of his stewardship, who can doubt that the Lord greeted him with, "Well done, good and faithful servant, enter thou into the joy of thy Lord."

What a festal welcome he must have received from thousands whom he had turned from darkness to light, from the power of Satan unto God, and who were now to become his crown of rejoicing in the presence of the Lord! These from the highland of Galatia, and those from the seaboard of Asia Minor. These from Judaistic prejudice, and those from the depths of Gentile depravity and sin. These from the degraded slave populations, and those from the ranks of the highborn and educated. Nor have such greetings ceased; but through all the centuries that have succeeded there are comparatively few that have passed along "the Way to the Celestial City" who have not had to acknowledge a deep debt of gratitude to him who, of all others, was enabled to give a clearer apprehension of the Divine method of justifying and saving sinners.